Writing
Audit
Reports

Mary C. Bromage

Second Edition

McGraw-Hill Book Company

New York   St. Louis   San Francisco
Auckland   Bogotá   Hamburg   Johannesburg
London   Madrid   Mexico   Montreal   New Delhi
Panama   Paris   São Paulo   Singapore
Sydney   Tokyo   Toronto

Library of Congress Cataloging in Publication Data

Bromage, Mary Cogan.
    Writing audit reports.

    Bibliography: p.
    Includes index.
    1. Auditors' reports. I. Title.
    HF5667.B762   1984   657'.452   83-25582
    ISBN 0-07-008064-X

    234567890 DOC/DOC 898765

ISBN 0-07-008064-X

*The editors for this book were William Sabin and Esther Gelatt,
the designer was Naomi Auerbach, and the production supervisor
was Reiko F. Okamura. It was set in Zapf Book by Byrd Data Imaging Group.*

Printed and bound by R. R. Donnelley & Sons Company.

To A.W.B.
in whom ethics and politics met

Contents

Preface

To practice what I preach, few words may be enough, but multiple thanks are due to those of you who make my work a pleasure. The thousands of auditors, as well as investigators and analysts in general, from both public and private sectors who have participated in my seminars on functional communication during recent years have taught me what really works in reporting on matters of urgent concern to our national well-being. Some are now leading authorities in their ever-developing profession. For such leaders primarily, the chapter on "Reviewing Drafts" has been added to this new edition of *Writing Audit Reports*.

Theories about "rules" for good writing are easy to preach in the university classroom. Putting principles to the test of everyday use is the real proof. What is classified merely as "correct" in writing may or may not lead to improved managerial operations, to reliable fiscal controls, and, in the last analysis, to just plain honesty of word, deed, and thought. Dollars and cents, as reported by the auditing profession, are inseparable from consideration of an organization's objectives, whether in business or in government.

Much responsibility for ethical values has been placed by public trust in the hands of your profession of auditing. As these values undergo change or, on occasion, subversion, auditors carry an increasing burden. Until academic training brings more of the realities of the outside world into the classroom, auditors who are seasoned (as well as schooled) by experience on the job must add their voices to the preparation necessary for turning out authenticated, convincing reports.

Without being an auditor but by being a practitioner of the written word, I have learned from others. They are auditors working in the field to which my present book is devoted. My earliest (and lasting) experience came from one of the "Big Eight" accounting firms and from the U.S. Army Audit Agency. Advice and counsel were freely sought from, and freely given by, many colleagues and other professional specialists, including among those many: Mr. Edgar E. Banbury, Professor R. Lee Brummet, Professor Robert L. Dixon, Mr. Richard C. Edris, Professor Alfred L. Edwards, Professor William K. Frankena, Mrs. Linda C. Graf, Mr. Thomas C. Green, Mr. William R. Hindman, Mr. Ivan D. Huelle, Mr. John H. Huston, Mr. Fred Kalhammer, Professor Walter G. Kell, Mr. Paul V. Koehly, Professor Michael W. Maher, Mr. Leo

Milner, Mr. Peter L. Orsburn, Ms. Marilyn Popyk, Mr. Murray H. Schofel, Mr. Robert Shanklin, Professor Donald H. Skadden, Professor W. Allen Spivey, Mr. Robert E. Wells, Professor James E. Wheeler, and Mr. James K. Wright. The staff members, past and present, of the Department of Agriculture, Interagency Auditor Training Programs, have brought into focus for many of us our mutual interests. My additional thanks are due to the Division of Research at the University of Michigan's School of Business Administration.

To all of you who pursue the unending search for precise and persuasive communication on paper, please read what I have written not as rules and regulations but as policies and procedures (to borrow your own words). Rule books themselves, as well as dictionaries, are of course essential.

What you will find here is an updating of language usage for our evolutionary times. Communication, as an expression of human behavior, cannot be rule-bound to the extent of becoming hidebound. It must, nevertheless, be based on commonly understood principles which tradition has proved worth retaining over the years. After all, in the working world, language is as language does. Your policies about tone, sequence, and style are, in part, your own individual determination; they are also determined by the particular organization and the special profession on behalf of which you have chosen to write.

Your report or other written document becomes your end product. It is the basis of how you and those whom you represent will be judged. To make this highly visible product a matter of personal and professional pride, technique (not mystique) is yours for the reading.

MARY C. BROMAGE
Professor Emerita
Graduate School of Business Administration
The University of Michigan

1984, Ann Arbor, Michigan

Introduction

Clarity and objectivity are long-avowed aims of functional writers including those in accounting. As these two attributes are now carried over into operational auditing, and into management studies in general, additional skills are demanded. The end product of functional writing, a formal report, is expected to be direct, concise, objective, verifiable, convincing, and (what is more) interesting.

Such goals cannot be achieved by the amateur, either as writer or as auditor. They depend on the acquisition of techniques in the communication process. Not all students of business necessarily prepare themselves to be skilled in English. Some years ago the *Journal of Accountancy* laid down the challenge for the auditing profession:

> ...it has discovered what a truly specialized accounting graduate the universities were turning out.... Lacking in broad business and economic concepts, weak in communication skills and unaware of the interrelationships of the other social and behavioral sciences, this graduate is not presently prepared for the new challenge.[1]*

Journalists, copywriters, editors, public relations experts—such specialists have long been expected to be trained in the use of language. Persons going into business have not regarded themselves as potential authors. As one senior federal auditor put it, " ...the accounting or

---

*Superior numbers refer to Notes at the end of the chapter.

1

business administration student is a different breed of cat from the liberal arts student."

Now the question is: Can such specialists become authors? Can they add to their professional qualifications the knack of communicating effectively on paper? For those willing to recognize practical writing as a discipline in itself, the tools are available that will give both speed and confidence. Functional writing is an acquired skill, not an inspired art—a matter of technique, not mystique.

THREE-WAY APPROACH

For a management analyst to write a successful report, three aspects of the undertaking must be mastered: "situation," "organization," and "style." Reports in, or allied to, auditing may be financial, operational, investigative, or consultative in nature. Whether the term "audit report" is regarded in its strictly financial sense or in its expanded sense, its author is now expected to be a professional in writing.

The *situation* leading up to the report includes reconciliation of the divergent roles of writer and reader. The auditor's purpose, that of determining certification or examining compliance or inducing operational changes, carries with it the necessity of pointing out a problem which the recipient may not, initially, be predisposed to welcome. Though the auditor has a captive audience, it is not always an acquiescent one.

Once the difficulties inherent in the relationship between author and reader are recognized, decisions are still to be faced about systematizing what has to be said. Good *organization* depends upon a sequence that will be logical and emphatic enough to be followed by the readers without confusion or uncertainty.

With situational factors confidently in hand, and with an orderly outline in mind, the auditor is ready to translate thinking into words, sentences, and paragraphs. What is needed is a *style* that seems simple and yet substantial; that is specific and yet safeguarded. The desire is to express factual observations, specific opinions, and feasible recommendations in language that is quickly comprehensible to all intended readers.

Such a threefold approach involves certain technical skills in psychology (situational factors), logic (organizational considerations), and language (stylistic principles). Writing is, after all, a form of human behavior, which rests on more than a rule book.

RELIANCE ON FORMAL REPORTING

In government and business, certain groups write more formal reports today than others: Professional auditors make up one of these groups, including those regarded as "financial" and those regarded as "operational," and also including those called "internal" and those called "external." Another related group consists of management consultants, often in public accounting firms. They rely on the report medium for recording "operational studies" and for proposing possible changes to those doing the actual managing of public or private affairs. Accountants and others holding responsible positions in managing the concerns of the everyday world also send other types of communications, but the formal report is their end product.

It is the accountant who is traditionally responsible for reviewing, analyzing, and transmitting "findings" and "opinions" related to disclosing, correcting, or improving management's performance. The formal document represents tangible proof of the effort, the proof which is prepared as a record of the work that has been done.

What constitutes this formal document? The earmarks are thorough content, including analytical judgments and supported inferences as well as facts: a systematic, established format; an orderly (usually predetermined) sequence; objectivity of style; sometimes, standardized phraseology prescribed by professional bodies; and, customarily, multiple distribution. The authors and the audience range from technical specialists to the chief officers of organizations, both corporate and civic. Typically, though not always, it is upward-directed, carrying with it a tradition of seriousness and materiality. Often, the document is available to the public. Because of established usage, its very appearance is likely to be familiar to sender and receiver, whether in a precast "short form" or in a longer version.

Because auditors have from the start depended on the painstaking medium of writing for communicating the results of their work, they have had a major influence on the form which the modern report now exhibits. In the evolutionary process, the form prescribed[2] for certification was not suited to evaluation of overall objectives, regulatory compliance, program goals, or management's general performance. The management letter of the Certified Public Accountant (CPA) provides one answer to that need. Today's formal report that has evolved for expanded coverage may serve present needs, but today's form will not necessarily suffice tomorrow.

Flexibility is matched by the need for familiarity. Valuable as these two assets are, they are partially self-contradictory: Familiarity implies holdover from the past, whereas flexibility implies incorporation of new approaches. The writer must adapt the reporting vehicle to every message without confusing the reader by erratic presentations. The document used by accountants in attesting to the financial accountability of an organization, best known in the short form, is not subject to change in many government and corporate affairs. The wording of opinions may vary, such as "unqualified," "qualified," or "adverse," or they may be "disclaimers."

AUDIT—GROWTH OF THE TERM

Because of rapid expansion in the examination of government and business affairs, the word "auditor" means different things to different people. Merriam-Webster's *Third New International Dictionary* (unabridged) says "auditor" means (in addition to "one that hears or listens") "one authorized to examine and verify accounts." "Audit" itself is defined as "a formal or official examination and verification of books of account. . . ."

The dictionary reflects history, whereas usage reflects currency. Whoever makes most use of a word is likely to control its sense. Usage changes. The attesting function remains within the exclusive jurisdiction of the duly qualified auditor. However, federal and state auditors are not engaged solely in certification, nor are they even primarily so engaged at times. They are examining operations of official agencies for compliance with regulations and fulfillment of objectives. Management consultants, often partners in CPA firms, are examining general operations at the request of management for the sake of meeting corporate objectives. They must comply with strict regulations.

The question is: Who has actually "authorized" the persons whom the dictionary has defined as auditors today? If they are CPAs, as is frequently but not uniformly the case, their employment by clients for the certification process might be regarded as the authorization. If they are not CPAs, as is now sometimes true for studies not leading to certification, the authorization arises from the organization which assigns the task.

Here, the restricted meaning takes on new connotations. Behind many reports called "audits," whether in the public or private sector, the purpose is that of advising management regarding deficiencies in operation or performance that may involve violations or inadequacies of publicly or privately imposed criteria.

Certain findings that cover more than fiscal certification are incorporated in management letters. Originally these were letters and carried that appearance, with selective content calling attention to needs for operational improvements as indicated by the financial statements. As the prevailing technological, social, and ethical environment made such needs increasingly apparent, many CPA firms formalized their services for management. "Some management consulting engagements bear a comparability to operational audits— particularly survey type engagements."[3] Formal reports are now issued in response to requests for advisory recommendations.

In about the middle of the twentieth century, federal agencies extended their audit function to include overall operations or performance. Auditors in many states also began to issue reports wherein recommendations, rather than certification, were the primary aim.

The Comptroller General of the United States in the early 1970s discussed the extension of governmental reviews to matters of economy and efficiency: " ... the most immediate need is in the area of State and local Governments, including work performed for them by public accountants. They must raise their sights to the level of determining how effective these programs really are. ... "[4]

Descriptions of the enlarged accounting function vary in connotation in both governmental and business affairs. The "internal" staff may be termed "reviewers," "inspectors," or "investigators" (seldom "consultants"). In its connotation versus its denotation, the term "auditor" does not now necessarily involve certification. Some reports issued from CPA firms are not written with that in view. Many governmental reports published under the rubric "audit" have effectiveness and efficiency as their target. Thus, the term "expanded" scope applies. There is such an expression as "the social audit," in which certification does not enter into the picture. The responsibility for attesting to the fairness of financial statements remains by ethical and regulatory control in the hands of the authorized independent auditor-accountant (the CPA).

"Auditing," as the term is used across the board, means that consideration of financial criteria, directly or indirectly, is part of the evaluative process. Some reports may take into account matters other than those involving income and expenditures, such as systems, procedures, contracts, compliance with regulations, and other operational aspects affecting the fulfillment of designated objectives. Sixty years ago, Arthur Young (of Arthur Young & Co.) is reported to have made this statement indicating the scope of CPA practice: " ... what you have asked from us is not an accountant's report, but our business judgment on the entire business situation."[5] In 1929, a pamphlet on audits, issued even earlier through the American Institute of Certified Public Accountants (AICPA), was revised by the Institute with the notation that earlier versions had been criticized by some CPAs for being "more comprehensive than their conception of the so-called balance-sheet audit" and by other CPAs for not bringing out "all the desired information."[6] But the pertinence of financial probity (to any enterprise) cannot be ignored so far as public and professional opinion understands the implications of the words "audit," "auditing," "auditor," and, even more recently, "auditee" (the entity audited).

Management itself is being analyzed either by self-initiation or by regulation. The purpose is to check financial reliability and also to assist in fulfilling its organizational goals, whether they consist of service, profit, or both and whether they are financial, social, economic, or all three in character. Although auditors are no longer regarded as a "bunch of bookkeepers with green eyeshades," they cannot relinquish their fiscal discipline.

So long as financial factors are included as either the primary or the supplementary testing basis, the report is usually called an "audit report." For an official definition of the word "audit," the glossary published in 1981 by the United States General Accounting Office gives this:

A term used to describe not only work done by accountants and auditors in examining financial statements, but also work done in reviewing (1) compliance with laws and regulations, (2) economy and efficiency of operations, and (3) effectiveness in achieving program results.[7]

The money aspect is not the sole standard of judgment in a report on overall accomplishment. Not all agree as to the wisdom of using the term "auditor" when referring to the enlarged scope of reviewing organizational performance: "A lot of people wish they [that is, auditors] would go back to checking expense vouchers and others grumble that they do not always dig deep enough. . . ."[8] Actually, the subjects under audit run the gamut of management's undertakings today.

The Director of the Office of Policy and Special Studies in the General Accounting Office (GAO) foresaw in 1970 what might be coming: "The auditor of financial statements, if he is doing his job properly, will find himself on much of the same ground as this so-called operational auditor."[9] When programs themselves are reviewed, their relationship to expenditure is an inescapable measure of adequacy. Today, functions described as "investigation," "analysis," "review," "internal auditing," "inspection," and "consulting" may also be included: "If it comes as a surprise that audit is a program evaluation process, one should understand that one of the program objectives of an accounting function is the accurate recording and reporting of income and expenditures and of assets and liabilities."[10]

At the same time that public bodies broadened their scope of review, there was a turn of events in public accounting. The larger CPA firms formed management advisory services under the direction of specially designated partners. Through these partners, at first exclusively CPAs, clients and others in business could request suggestions concerning their "across the board" operations.

Differences exist between the reports prepared by federal or state audit agencies and those submitted in management consulting engagements. In CPA firms, the management consultants' early reports (in the 1960s) resembled the familiar management letters, sometimes sent to corporate clients at the time of regular fiscal audits:

Management services rendered by CPAs present an area of practice in which growth is limited only by the CPA's ability to solve problems and create confidence in his judgment. As the population explosion creates greater competition in the business and financial worlds, the need for management services will grow.[11]

The management consultant's role differs from that of the government auditor. It differs also from that of the external auditor and that of the internal auditor. The differences are attributable to the respective relationships between the consultant and the client and between the auditor and the auditee. The former is voluntary, coming into being on request only, and the written product is not typically labeled an "audit report." In the auditor's case, the assignment is usually conducted in accordance with an obligation of the marketplace, as one leading accountant puts it,[12] representing an involuntary relationship as far as the recipient is concerned. Whether the Securities and Exchange Commission (SEC) required it or not, a company would seek clarification for the sake of its competitive status. This is, as one lawyer explained: ". . . a time when auditors are subject to a staggering number of lawsuits, [and] intense pressures from managements to adopt accounting treatments that will put the best face on the financial statements. . . ."[13]

The auditors must preserve their independence with no option but to review and record negative conditions such as noncompliance or fiscal irregularities. They must at the minimum audit fiscal matters. The consultant, as such, reviews and reports only to the client on the request basis. True, the former's report now goes beyond the negative into positive recommendations. The consultant, as is no less true, does not exclude financial implications. Herein lies the resemblance of the roles, made increasingly obvious in the content and format of their end product, the report itself.

Yet the time has not come for complete similarity in the reports. The independent auditors can in no sense join the team of the company, the firm, the agency, or the project being audited. Nor can the consultants work hand in glove with the client so as to make themselves one with the client's management.

Broadened coverage has developed both from the regulatory point of view and from the operational point of view: ". . . some call it investigating, the G.A.O. prefers 'auditing' and still others say it is prying."[14] In concentrating on the expansion of operational implications and the influence upon the form of reporting, the writers themselves must exercise all due professional caution.

AIMS IN REPORTS

Financial and operational auditing is intended to give notice of management's conformance with recognized requirements. The formal report itself is the only evidence of the independent auditor's completed analysis. In many such presentations the purpose is not merely to certify or inform, necessary as that may be. Nor does the ultimate aim stop with making recommendations. Not until constructive changes ("corrective actions") have actually been put into effect by the recipient, eliminating deficiencies, can the writer feel the ultimate goal has been achieved.

An audit fulfills its overall purpose first by pointing out deficiencies and inefficiencies. But it may not be enough to determine that moneys have been lost, that staff hours have been wasted, or that benefits have been lacking. Only when the author convinces the reader that such problems can be solved can the report be said to have succeeded. Success is now furthered by the trend toward commenting on the favorable points as well as the obligatory identification of the unfavorable.

NOTES

[1] Arthur E. Witte, "Management Auditing: The Present State of the Art," *Journal of Accountancy*, vol. 124, no. 2, August 1967, p. 57.

[2] See American Institute of Certified Public Accountants, *Statement on Auditing Standards*, no. 1, par. 511.04, New York, 1973, p. 81.

[3] W. R. Hindman, CPA, letter to author, Apr. 17, 1975.

[4] Elmer B. Staats, "Governmental Auditing in a Period of Rising Social Concerns," address, Nassau, 1972. (Pamphlet.)

[5] Quoted in L. C. J. Yeager and Gordon Ford, *History of the Professional Practice of Accounting in Kentucky*, Courier-Journal Lithographing Company, Louisville, Ky., 1968, p. 14.

[6] AICPA, *Statement on Auditing Standards*, app. A, p. 200.

[7] United States General Accounting Office, *Standards for Audit of Governmental Organizations, Programs, Activities, and Functions*, 1981 Revision, Government Printing Office, Washington, p. 63.

[8] Linda Charlton, "Inquiry in Democratic Break-In Strips General Accounting Office of Some of Its Anonymity," *The New York Times*, Sept. 3, 1972. © 1972 by The New York Times Company. Reprinted by permission.

[9] Ellsworth H. Morse, Jr., "Performance and Operational Auditing," *Journal of Accountancy*, vol. 131, no. 6, June 1971, p. 41.

[10] Reprinted with the permission of the National Association of College and University Business Officers (NACUBO) from the July 1973 *Studies in Management*, "Program Review and Evaluation in the Business and Financial Area," by Wilbur K. Pierpont, p. 1.

[11] Yeager and Ford, *History of the Professional Practice . . .* , p. 132.

[12] Donald H. Skadden, The University of Michigan, discussion with author, 1978.

[13] Douglas W. Hawes, quoted in *The New York Times*, Apr. 14, 1974. © 1974 by The New York Times Company. Reprinted by permission.

[14] *The New York Times*, Sept. 3, 1972. © 1972 by The New York Times Company. Reprinted by permission.

1 Choosing words

Words bother people. Writers have their likes and dislikes, and readers have theirs; is it possible to satisfy both? From the half million or more words contained in the largest American dictionary, auditors need to select those best suited for each particular report. In carrying out this task they may wonder, at times: Why write at all? At the exit conference, why not just say what has been found and have done with it? Actual detection of the deficiencies could well consume the allotted workdays. On the receiving end, some would prefer not having criticisms placed on the record.

In preparing a formal report, not only word choice presents problems; so do sentence structure and paragraph development. Knowledge of rules and changing usage is involved in reducing matters to writing. Until that ultimate phase of reporting is accomplished, however, there is no assurance of permanence or precision. Neither is there assurance that the right recipients have been informed.

OBJECTIVES

At least three reasons justify the extra investment of time and labor required to put the findings on paper: permanence, precision, and pinpointing. All involve word choice.

Permanence

A report is proof positive and proof permanent that certain facts have been observed, and comments thereon delivered. Professional responsibilities are at stake. One partner in a certified public accounting firm emphasized the point that: "... our report is for documentation for posterity of what has already been accomplished."[1] If the reporting process ended with suggestions made during the course of discussing an organization or a program, or even with the exit conference, who would there be to prove or disprove disparities in recalling what had been said? Underlining the need for a readily accessible written reference is the "repeat" engagement that reiterates conditions remaining in spite of apparent concurrence by management.

Precision

A second reason for a report is the need for exactitude: "... the profession has worked long and hard to establish standardized phraseology having precise meaning...."[2] By contrast, the spoken word offers less opportunity for planning how much or how little to include. Random instances may come to a speaker's mind instead of selected, representative, balanced data. Hence the old saying, "I could have bitten my tongue off." Off-the-cuff comments cannot be predetermined as to scope. It is easier to control the direction of coverage on paper.

The chance for precision comes from the chance to revise wording itself. Replacement of an ambiguous expression, qualification of an absolute term, or support for a subjective implication is the special privilege of the writer, a privilege and an obligation. One vice-president banned "presently" in favor of "currently" on the grounds that "presently" does not necessarily mean "currently"; it may mean "soon." For the functional communicator, being exact is worth what one creative author, the poet T. S. Eliot, called "the intolerable wrestle with words and meanings."[3] When the content of a report by its very nature is likely to be resisted, the acceptability and comprehensibility of its wording are crucial. Notwithstanding all efforts, "... users of financial statements continue to misunderstand or fail to understand what an auditor's report says and does not say."[4]

Pinpointing

Vocabulary is one means whereby writers adapt their information to those obligated to receive it, whether few or many. As with permanence and precision, pinpointing the designated recipients transfers the responsibility for action to those in charge of managing an enterprise, whether the management relationship is "internal" or "external."

The trend in pinpointing is decidedly outward, not inward. "Disclosure" is the expression heard more often than "confidentiality." Yet disclosure is a problem in the minds of senders and receivers alike, a problem which makes the pressure upon matters of terminology all the greater. Even when a report is intended for limited circulation, confidentiality of content is becoming increasingly difficult. Politically, the question of controlling the flow of information is a sensitive one. In federal government reports the Freedom of Information Act of 1966 (P.L. 89-487, as amended subsequently, including the 1967 P.L. 9-23, Title V, U.S. Code, Sec. 552) compels many writers to reconsider their audience. The act has special implications for investigators and researchers.

In addressing those and only those who can be counted upon to agree, there is little ground for worry. For some who can be counted on to disagree, words provide a highly visible target. When a report gets into the newspapers, the reaction of the readers is incalculable. As profit or nonprofit organizations grow in size and sensitivity of their programs, products, personnel, sales, or services, the public's desire to know expands. Whether the recipients are one or a million, there are many whose reactions rest upon how a report is attuned to them individually.

With the auditor's commitment to the written medium, the end result is the formalized document, worded in such a way that it will accomplish its special purposes. Though extensive standardization has been required for financial audits, a challenge is posed by the diversified operations that have to be covered in a broadened scope.

VOCABULARY SOURCES

Inadequate vocabulary is a general concern of all practitioners of communication, along with their fear of being either too vague or too explicit, too formal or too informal, too wordy or too blunt.

Such difficulties are compounded by the rate at which new terms are being coined, a rate said to have been equaled only during the Renaissance, a period, like the present, filled with invention and exploration: "Always, as men have met with new objects and new experiences and have developed new ideas, they have needed new words to describe them."[5] "Transthetics" was invented in 1977 by engineers and architects, working together in a large company, to fill a slot in the language when they wanted to refer to the aesthetic facilities being designed for transmitting power. It may or may not reach dictionary status. Another new word, "auditee," familiar in professional publications, has been slow to win lexicographers' recognition. The term "robotics" reached some dictionaries in 1981, as did "byte."

The size of the average individual's vocabulary today is a wide-open question:

> There are cynical souls who claim the average man actively uses no more than 600 or 700 words. Others would assign an active vocabulary of 25,000 and a passive vocabulary of up to 100,000 to the well-educated and culturally oriented person. We know of no estimate that is more than an educated guess.[6]

With all the riches of contemporary language, report-writers need more words in the memory bank than they habitually use.

Just like money in a savings account, words are not so much for expenditure as for reserve in time of need. Keeping pocket notebooks in which to jot down the new or meaningful terms appearing in reputable periodicals is one way to increase the supply. Learning words by their derivation constitutes a history of the times, present as well as past. Crossword puzzles are for the most resourceful word fans. Electronic games may provide another stimulus.

Report-writers draw from their working environment as well as from dictionaries and other resources. Colorful, emotional language is not part of that working environment. Multisyllabled, little-known terminology is out. Pretentious, pseudo-profound, unusual, "literary" language is not suitable. The style must be familiar, objective, and safeguarded so as to be recognized on sight by all intended readers, from the best informed to the least.

Language is a map to the territory it is supposed to represent,[7] a territory that is expanding. No matter how extensive the verbal resources, professional demands prescribe a certain amount of specialization and standardization, with a maximum amount of condensation and clarification.

SPECIALIZATION

Vocabularies become extremely technical. This trend is at once an asset and a liability. "Jargon," as such usage is called by many, is a professional necessity, but it can become a professional hazard. To name one field, there are thousands of names for chemical compounds with which only the chemist is conversant. The question concerns not the justification of jargon (literally defined as "the twittering of birds") but its usefulness. The answer lies with the reader; the mere fact that the writer understands is not enough.

Auditors, like scientists, engineers, lawyers, and others, acquire their own private terminologies. There is no doubt as to the existence of audit jargon; the doubt is only as to its serviceability. Two considerations are at stake:

1. Recognition of one's own jargon
2. Familiarity to one's reader.

Writers' recognition

On the first of the two points, audit terminology arises not from one specialty but from accounting, electronic data processing, systems work, taxation, statutory and administrative regulations, and the diversity of all the entities audited.

For most auditors, the language of accounting and finance has become second nature. On this score the American Institute of Certified Public Accountants (AICPA) stipulates that: "The practitioner must be able to reach all levels and act as an expert 'translator,' rendering technical language and complex concepts into plain English. He must write for the reader and avoid technical jargon."[8] Auditors do not typically report to other auditors. Expressions like:

... deobligate

... expense an item

... in-kind costs

... shortfall

... fixed and variable costs

make specific sense to the CPA but leave others confused.

The problem goes beyond accountants: "The world of corporate management ... is not the world of the average person. The vocabulary of that world is not his or her vocabulary. The terms 'bottom line' and 'capital formation,' so important to corporate management, are the problems of 'making ends meet.' ..."[9] Even less familiar than financial language is that of data processing because it is not as old. Developments in such a dynamic field are so rapid that their linguistic description may be not only familiar but also ridiculed, as one company found when it announced its forthcoming production of "an intelligent terminal." Specialists who use shoptalk outside the shop are accused of speaking gobbledygook. What is worse, the genuineness of their desire to communicate is suspect.

The way to escape such suspicion is to be aware when jargon is jargon. Auditors are exposed to many kinds. For those in the know, a specialized word, whatever its source, is both quick and precise. Expressions peculiar to the subjects under review (military, industrial, environmental, contractual, and so forth) are already diverse, with more being added as the operations under review multiply. One whole set of words, like "prime sponsor" and "subgrantee," accompanies the audit of grant moneys. Contract audits have their peculiarities; here the "contractor" is referred to not as a human being but as a corporate body. Auditors inevitably lapse into the idiom they hear from their clients.

Caution has to be exercised in deciding how much of the idiom can be carried onto paper. "Loess" appeared in an examination of funding of a proposed building's site. Though common parlance among soil experts, the meaning (an unstratified deposit of loam) proved unknown to most of the company's officers. "Adsorption," appearing in connection with a scientific experiment, was not a misprint, as one reader assumed, but was the correct (if unfamiliar) word for adherence to a surface. In analyzing a system, one writer carried over for general use the word "triage" without explaining that it relates to the classification of patients for priority of care. "Layer operation" as used in another report referred to chicken farming. "Ergonomics" in a finding about the operation of a motorcycle related to its controls. "Problem paper" was employed without further specification in regard to a credit association's deficiencies.

Essential as it is to learn the specialist's own lingo in the information-gathering phase, familiarization subjects the reporting medium to the risk of unintelligibility to outsiders. Writers forget that they, too, had to ask what something meant when they first heard it.

Newness itself may render words objectionable. The "-izing" of old words, convenient as it has proved, incurs scorn from some; "finalize" was one of the first, along with the now frequently used "maximize" and "minimize." From there the practice has spread to "prioritize," "dollarize," "inferioritize," "customize," "randomize," "digitize," "cannibalize," and "computerize." If there is no short substitute already in existence, such a process has to take place, like it or not. The next step is "prioritization" and "dollarization," already appearing in some reports. Noah Webster, writing to a friend in 1817, foretold this course of events: " . . . a living language must keep pace with improvement and knowledge and with the multiplication of ideas."[10] An old word may move to a new status:

Subordinate installations were not tasked to report their activities.

"Tasked"? By a kind of structural jargon, nouns become adjectives— "electricity supply board"; nouns become verbs—"to access the computer," "to trend the loans," "to format the information"; verbs that are commonly active (where the subject is the doer of the action) become passive (where the subject is the receiver of the action)—"procedures must be conformed with requirements"; nouns become both verbs and adjectives—"to impact upon" and "impactful"; and verbs become nouns—"If errors exist, the program proceeds to the next compare."

Grammar books and readers' tastes differ about such slides, but words are on the move. When all the authorities have been consulted and all is said and done, the final choice comes right back to the communicator, a choice that cannot be made solely on the basis of individual preference.

Readers' comprehension

Once specialists recognize that they think and talk in their own idioms, their written output poses questions of clarity and acceptability to the full audience. Even though new terms may be defined in the latest dictionary, readers do not read with that volume in hand. One auditor, in presenting findings, gave a helpful introductory comment:

> We consider the costs determined by the regular accountant to be "record costs," and the costs determined by the budget control accountant to be "accrued expenditures."

In view of the range of those entitled to have access to reports, there are obvious advantages to plain, commonly understood wording. The publicity which official audits receive is reason enough to use such a style. Writers get walled in by the compartments within which they work. The danger is that outsiders see things differently: "A research staff member of the Institute of Chartered Accountants of Scotland reports that, in the study of the word 'depreciation,' to ascertain just what it meant he found 24 different interpretations in accounting literature. So what can a layman expect?"[11] Writers dealing with progressively specialized material may have to define and illustrate when simple synonyms do not exist.

The principle that controls the choice between the particular or the plain word is the nature of the reader, not the nature of the writer. No word or set of words is perfect. Some degree of translation is always involved.

In regard to technical terms, the first warning to writers is to be aware that their terms may, indeed, be technical. Writers may fail to realize when they are "speaking Greek." The second warning is to resist the tempting but often unfounded assumption that readers will know what is meant. Solutions lie in:

- Recognizing when a word is specialized
- Not overassuming readers' familiarity
- Employing words in common use if possible
- Signaling special meanings by quotation marks

- Defining uncommon expressions
- Including a glossary
- Adding examples to pin down definitions.

STANDARDIZATION

Standardization of vocabulary can be helpful. On the positive side, use of the same expression for the same purposes decreases the likelihood of misinterpretation: "Absolute standardization is desirable so that every auditor communicates exactly the same message to every reader."[12] Agreed-upon formulas also accelerate the writing as well as the reading time. On the negative side, readers who sense repetitious wording skim over it without really applying it to the immediate point. The content then does not register in their minds.

Formalized wording has proved feasible chiefly for the short-form financial audits. Over the years auditing, like legal practice and other professional activities, has inculcated conformity for safety's sake.

The stereotyped phraseology of financial reports has influenced operational reports, even where the subject matter and the breadth of review call for variation. Each new program brings with it expressions not derived from previous subjects. Whether to seek variation or to utilize previous wording is a decision that will be influenced by the formality or the informality of the tone desired.

Degrees of formality

Formality in the full sense implies rule-book English, itself a form of standardization. Such devices as contractions ("don't," "won't," "let's," "'til," "it's") are not the tradition in reporting. Personal pronouns are used sparingly in such writing except for the third person ("he," "she," "it," or "they," for instance). Auditors practically never use the first person singular ("I," "me," "my," or "mine") but do rely upon the first person plural ("we," "us," "our," and "ours"), especially in drawing conclusions and making recommendations. Investigators, at times, may have to report by means of "I," "me," or "my" for purposes of verifiability. The plural versus the singular reflects a team effort rather than a solo voice. "You" as the second person pronoun, appearing occasionally, is implied if the imperative verb (giving a direction or command) is used, as in "Add":

> The weight of the helicopter, two crew members, and engine oil totals 5,210 pounds. Add the maximum allowable gross weight of 4,000 pounds for the cargo....Now the maximum takeoff gross weight of 9,000 pounds for the helicopter is exceeded by 210 pounds.

Adherence to conventions in language, like adherence to conventions in manners or dress, constitutes one way of approaching people. With wording, it is the tone that tells its own story. The very concept of formal reporting entails a distinct style. Formality usually arises from awareness that a certain "distance" intervenes between senders and receivers. As a situational control factor, distance may consist of geographical miles, organizational hierarchies, cultural expectations, or professional objectives.

Between writers and readers whose interests are identical, informality is more natural. Between persons growing up in the same cultural environment, there is less need for linguistic rituals, some of which are time- and paper-consuming. To make the tone conversational, informality is growing in the communications of most professions.

Most important among the considerations in choosing between a formal and an informal style is the separating factor of different objectives. In an advisory report, writers hope for action on a deficiency, whereas it is the recipient's hope to be above criticism. Informality arising naturally out of similarity of objectives and out of personal contact, may prove ineffectual if carried too far. Preserving a safe distance, yet not seeming remote or aloof, is accomplished by keeping some but not all of the formalities.

The write-up of audits has historically been nonconversational, tightly defined, and thereby safeguarded, but at the same time it has been repetitive and trite. Such changes as are now taking place require watchful but open-minded consideration by both the drafters and their reviewers who make up the reporting task force. Suitability for the readers constitutes the criterion. As pomposity goes, courtesy and respect need not vanish.

A noticeable trend toward less formality is the replacing of legalistic (and often unnecessary) phrases such as "the following" and "as follows." Smoother linking is provided by the colon itself:

The accounts were arranged in order:

    Checking

    Savings

    Trust.

Such conventions as mechanical references to "the above matter" can be carried to the extent of slowing up the reader. Where is "the above matter"? Is it really "above" or some pages back? Similar difficulty comes from "the items below." If a reader needs reminding of something that has already been mentioned, or forewarning of something that is to come, the wording should be substantive, as it would be in talking: "the financial matters" or "the five items listed for inclusion."

Once the tight muscles of old style are relaxed, writers sound less like automatons and more like people, as in one passage dealing with time-and-effort studies:

> ...2½ hours shy of full time.

"Shy" is an apt, short word. On the same page several other "spoken" expressions (colloquialisms) occurred:

> ...more scientific standards than the ups and downs of sales.
>
> Neither fish nor fowl, the Guarantee Program lies somewhere between the two.

Without throwing overboard entirely the expected formalities, the sound, if not the casualness, of the spoken word is gradually being adopted. Though it is unrealistic to "write as you talk" altogether, it is time to advocate writing that is more like talking. Telephone, radio, and television make this era resound with oral input. In the trend toward less formality, one caution concerns the necessity for retaining control through well-defined meanings, whether technical or general, formal or informal, standardized, or original.

Definitions

Defining may be the solution, as one data processor demonstrated for the specialized word "ego-less":

> The concept of ego-less programming is based upon programmer teams that perform structured walk-through of all or most of the programs they are developing.

To make sure that terms dealing with particular financial areas convey the right meaning, public accounting firms sometimes include, from time to time, explanations:

> Blocked accounts. Bank accounts in moneys within a country that are restricted by the monetary authorities....

Recently, "throughput" was given a particularized definition by the International Accountants Society, Inc., of Chicago: "...productivity based on all the facets of an operation; for example, a computer with capability of simultaneous operations."[13] The same word remains generalized in Merriam-Webster's *Third New International Dictionary* (unabridged): "an amount of raw material put through processing or finishing operations in a specific time." "Zero-suppression" is "elimi-

nation of nonsignificant zeroes in a numeral."[14] "Outcollect" was used
to describe the transactions of an island-based telephone company in
reference to a ticket that represented a call which was placed on a
collect basis but which was referred to a continental location for
billing. Without any synonym, a sentence was required to define it, a
sentence worth its space. To define well is not easy; mental discipline
has to be exerted to control terminology.

The various kinds of opinions that can be rendered by a CPA have
been controlled by the definitions of the AICPA. For the sake of
common interpretation, codification rules out loose implication. Not
only is the "short form" (in contrast to the "long form") defined as
being that "customarily used in connection with basic financial
statements," but recommended phrasing for the different forms has
been adopted by the Institute for the sake of "reasonable uniformity."[15]

So that denotation (the direct and specific meaning of a word) will
prevail over connotation (the implied meaning), advance definitions
are useful. Yet it is hard to legislate interpretation. One federal
regulatory commission instructed private agencies coming within its
jurisdiction that:

> The agencies' rules must contain language substantially similar to or
> identical to that which is found in the . . . Commission's criteria set forth in
> Section Number . . . of the regulations.

The only way to prevent misunderstanding of some words is to
establish meanings common to user and receiver. Such definitions
involve context because context itself is part of the reading process. No
word is an island. Defining extends, for that reason, to whole phrases.

Common words as well as specialized ones may need explanation:

> The 343 requisitions were grouped into 46 cases (a case represents a
> transmittal of requisitions, regardless of number, from a contractor).

An old word may be used in a new sense, but new words, like
"flextime," "auditee," "detailee," and "environeering," are also being
coined to express new concepts. Since such terms get into use before
they appear in dictionaries, the user has to explain them.

To preclude unwanted connotations, the thought process must be
intensively applied. The term itself should not be incorporated in its
definition, of course, or what is already unclear becomes more so as
happened in one official attempt:

> Subproject. A subproject is a project divided into subprojects. Subprojects
> are for use in connection with budget programming and execution. For
> accounting and reporting purposes, subprojects will be considered pro-
> jects.

Variation

If too much standardization creeps in, and there is such a thing as creeping standardization, the only change may consist in putting new figures and dates in last year's report. This may be one way of getting a draft through the editing process. The game is this: What worked before should work again. There are all-purpose passages:

> This report contains our recommendations for improvements.
>
> A table of contents is provided for each reference.
>
> The following items are of significance.

The portions most susceptible to triteness are the openings and closings:

> We have performed an audit. . . .

For a change, this might be better:

> We audited. . . .

Endings, as in a letter report, may also become routine:

> We have reviewed the subjects in this report with both the Director and his Assistant. After our comments have been considered, we would be pleased to discuss them with you.

Such formulas do save thinking on the part of the writers but do not produce much from the readers. All-purpose language loses its particular applicability. Words wear out their welcome. By contrast, advance planning of how to motivate the exact action desired makes that action more probable:

> . . . the next step in issuing the final report is to secure your reaction to the draft. We will call you to set the date when enough time has elapsed for your reading of the drafts.

Tailor-made wording is what works best in tailor-made audits of operations and programs.

One aspect of standardization is that certain wordsets must be used. Financial audits are hemmed in by legal and professional constraints; hence there is extensive similarity. CPAs are not free to make more than minor alterations in such time-honored passages as:

> In our opinion, the Statement of Budget fairly represents, in accordance with generally accepted accounting principles, the results of the contract cost for the period examined, subject to the questioned costs.

The "hard-core" inevitable in auditing, whether financial or operational, includes:

finding	conditions
recommendation	scope
opinion	background

Up to a point, such ritualistic language is expected. The amount of duplication that is required makes it all the more desirable to shun such words when they are not required.

Interestingly enough, it is not the nonreplaceable words that are repeated, but rather the common, garden-variety terms, which may appear over and over on one page, within one paragraph, and sometimes within one sentence:

> ...programs <u>developed</u> for the Department are <u>required</u> to meet the regulatory <u>requirements</u> applicable to the <u>required</u> operations that have been <u>developed</u>.

The underlined words can be replaced with synonyms or dropped:

> ...programs developed for the Department must meet regulations applicable to the required operations.

The frequency rate is high for certain favorites:

area	deficiency	please advise	need improvement
seems	disclosed	as a result	determine
also	in addition	significant	establish
feel	generally	problem area	appears
timely	based on	substantial	perform
proper	material	not always	adequate

The seeming inescapability of some of these words can make them habit-forming. Boredom is their effect, and a bored reader is not a responsive one. A word applied to too many situations soon means all things to all people.

One overworked favorite in some reports is "assure": in other reports it is "ensure," and occasionally "insure." The availability of all three, separated by a shade of meaning, offers the chance for more variation. Though the average person finds the distinction unnecessary (all three are defined as "to make certain"), the auditor can benefit by discriminating between them: "*Assure* refers to persons, and it alone has the sense of setting a person's mind at rest:..."[16] Strictly speaking, "assure" takes persons as the receivers of its action:

Local managers must assure themselves of the accuracy of the information.

"Ensure" takes things as the receiver of its action:

> The unliquidated obligations should be determined to ensure completeness of the project.

"Insure" connotes the guaranteeing of life or property against risks and generally seems less useful in auditing. Preservation of the fine line between the other two, however, will prevent overuse of either one.

Another reason for lack of variation is the recourse to "vogue" words, those which come into fashion because someone of prominence, a "fashion" leader, gives them a start. At best, they sound prestigious; at worst, pretentious. Each may be good in its own right, but when it is reiterated, the original relevance is lost:

parameter	continuum
escalate	thrust
exposure	posture
viable	perceive
challenging	generate

Less ostentatious alternatives are often more fitting. An "in" word ("scenario," for instance, or "synergistic") has a limited lifetime when it is worked to death. As an eighteenth-century poet wrote:

> In words as fashions, the same rule will hold,
> Alike fantastic if too new or old;
> Be not the first by whom the new are tried
> Nor yet the last to lay the old aside.[17]

Fairly or unfairly, a writer's limiting and imitating of vocabulary is taken as a limitation and imitation of thought. "Inkhorn" vocabulary comes through as just that: unnecessarily pedantic.

Lack of variation diminishes the communicative quality and quantity. Once writers decide to make reports interesting as well as precise and brief, they can get away from stereotyped wording. A dictionary or a thesaurus (literally, a treasure book of words) offers the way. Undesirable repetition occurs where there are options, not where professionalism hamstrings the auditor.

ADAPTATION

Operational reporting has not yet exhibited standardization to the degree seen in financial reporting. The very diversification of fields opens new possibilities. The lack of "models" demands more of the writers, requiring discretion to construct vocabulary strictly within the contextual sense and the readers' range. Auditors face choices as to formality or informality, denotations or connotations, and repetition or variation. Adapting language to current needs does not mean ignoring traditional essentials.

NOTES

[1] Murray H. Schofel, CPA, letter to author, Mar. 21, 1975.

[2] Philip L. Defliese, Kenneth P. Johnson, and Roderick K. MacLeod, *Montgomery's Auditing*, 9th ed., The Ronald Press Company, New York, 1975, p. 778.

[3] T. S. Eliot, "East Coker," *Four Quartets*, in *The Complete Poems and Plays: 1909–1950*, Harcourt Brace Jovanovich, Inc., New York, 1952, p. 125.

[4] Defliese et al., *Montgomery's Auditing*, p. 778.

[5] James Lowe, *6,000 Words: A Supplement to Webster's Third New International Dictionary*, Merriam-Webster Inc., Springfield, Mass., 1976, p. 132.

[6] By permission. From letter to author (Oct. 20, 1975) by G. & C. Merriam Company, Publishers of the Merriam-Webster Dictionaries.

[7] Samuel I. Hayakawa, *Language in Thought and Action*, Harcourt Brace Jovanovich, Inc., New York, 1972, p. 27.

[8] American Institute of Certified Public Accountants, Management Advisory Services, *Task Force on Evaluation of Efficiency and Program Results*, New York, May 1976, p. 62.

[9] John W. Hill, quoted in the *The New York Times*, Oct. 6, 1976. © 1976 by The New York Times Company. Reprinted by permission.

[10] By permission. From *Webster's Third New International Dictionary* © 1971 by G. & C. Merriam Co., Publishers of the Merriam-Webster Dictionaries.

[11] A. J. Watson, "Do Financial Statements Communicate?" *The Accountant's Magazine*, vol. 72, Edinburgh, May 1968, p. 236. With the permission of the Editor of *The Accountant's Magazine*.

[12] Defliese et al., *Montgomery's Auditing*, p. 744.

[13] International Accountants Society, Inc., *A Concise Dictionary of EDP Terms*, Chicago, undated, p. 20.

[14] General Automation, Inc., *Glossary of Commonly Used Computer Terms*, Santa Ana, California, undated.

[15] AICPA *Statement on Auditing Standards*, no. 1, pars. 511.02–511.03, New York, 1973, p. 81.

[16] *The American Heritage Dictionary of the English Language*, William Morris (ed.), American Heritage Publishing Co., Inc., and Houghton Mifflin Company, Boston, 1973, p. 80.

[17] Alexander Pope, "Essay on Criticism," in *The Complete Works of Alexander Pope*, Houghton Mifflin Company, Boston, 1903, p. 71.

2 Adapting vocabulary

Brevity has top priority today. New media are competing for attention, offering speedier transmission and lower cost. Electronic mail leads to quicker delivery and permits quicker intake. Writing, when it has to be the chosen instrument, will serve its purpose if held down in length. Though the one-page communication has undeniable appeal, formal reports require more. Cut, cut, cut is the way to achieve conciseness. If someone other than the originator does the deleting, the whole meaning may be distorted.

CONDENSATION

Verbosity constitutes an imposition. The minutes or hours it takes to get through a report become excessive when there is, among other deterrents, unclear abbreviation, outright gamesmanship, verbatim restatement, or obvious redundancy.

Abbreviations

Abbreviations that are clear result in economy of space and time on both sides of the communication fence. The quality that makes them good is their instant recognizability. The use of "K" for million and "M" or "m" for thousand is unclear to many readers. (An alternative to writing out "$3,000,000" or "$50,000" would be "$3 million" or "$50 thousand.") Even when internationally known, some, such as "%" for percent, are scarce in formal writing. If brevity is the turning point, "%" will gradually be accepted. Although a symbol may be generally understood, the fact that the author does not take the trouble to write it out may be regarded as a discourtesy.

Industry and government alike invent new shortcuts daily, driven to them by the complexity and frequency of their nomenclature:

GAO (General Accounting Office)

DoD (Department of Defense)

GNP (gross national product)

CPA (Certified Public Accountant)

MAS (management advisory service)

IBM (International Business Machines)

Brevity being the modern reader's loudest demand, more shortcutting seems in prospect. One characteristic of today's style is the acronym (a word formed from the initial letters of each of the major parts of a term): "VISTA," "snafu," "NASA," "laser," "radar." The word "scuba" originated as the acronym for "<u>s</u>elf-<u>c</u>ontained <u>u</u>nderwater <u>b</u>reathing <u>a</u>pparatus," though few remember the origin of the acronym.

Though clear to some readers, acronyms seem like "alphabet soup" to others. Within a closed network of co-workers, there is no uncertainty, but few reporting networks now remain closed. "Fifo" (first in, first out) and "lifo" (last in, first out) are beyond question in an accountant's mind and have entered the dictionary, but nonaccountants would still have to look them up. One of the most frequent complaints from readers is against acronyms. As in many aspects of communication, people like their own but heartily dislike the unfamiliar acronyms of others. A policy that would help business, as it has already done in government, would be to spell out the whole the first time the shortcut is used, with the abbreviation following in parentheses, and to use the abbreviated form thereafter. Without such a start, how will an outsider know whether AMA stands for the American Management Association, the American Marketing Association, or the American Medical Association? Another useful device is a glossary at the beginning.

The creation of acronyms and abbreviations daily is a sign of pressure on the communication process. The larger and the more intricate an organization, the more of these it spawns. Without such devices to take the place of whole words, reports would be longer and more repetitious. For all kinds of abbreviating, the loss through ambiguity has to be weighed against the gain through brevity.

Capital letters

The capitalizing not only of the first letter in a sentence but of abbreviations (some), acronyms, titles, headings, and proper names is mostly a rule-bound matter. The effect of an uppercase (capital) letter as opposed to a lowercase (small) letter is to create emphasis. The uppercase is eye-catching and should not be employed indiscriminately or it will weaken emphasis; the reader ceases to react. Twentieth-century American practice differs from older habits, when handwriting was more frequent than typing. Capital letters abound in nineteenth-century manuscripts. Even today, as handwriting is reviving in offices on account of its speed, drafters need to follow modern rules. Otherwise, the final typed version will emerge in random uppercase and lowercase letters. The signal given by a capital letter should be a clear-cut one, based on modern practice.

Gamesmanship

The games that writers play with words, either consciously or unconsciously, do not fool many nowadays. Fancy wording is regarded as just that:

> Management has asked for a medium whereby to garner a better understanding of data processing.

"Garner?" Why not "gain" or "acquire"? Words that are unnecessarily long may also be regarded as pretentious. The writer who inflates the language does not retain its true value.

Abstract wording often sidesteps the concrete and verifiable. Abstract words are needed for mental concepts, expressing categories of specific objects. Unavoidable abstractions (like "capital expenditures") can be offset by the concrete specification ("irrigation systems" and "cattle sheds"):

> The system is applied to financing large capital expenditures for such necessities as irrigation systems and cattle sheds.

One audit director was puzzled by the abstractness of a reference to the "location" in a draft submitted for his approval. "Location" might refer to any of many specific places:

> Unpredictable expenditures have occurred because of the location of the work.

The working paper (workpaper) showed that the project was conducted in Canada; the director sought for still more concreteness and found that the "location" was on Canada's Cumberland Peninsula between 65 and 68 degrees north latitude. The approved report was revised to read:

> Unpredictable expenditures may have been made because the work was conducted at the Arctic Circle on Baffin Island in Canada's Northwest Territories.

The piling up of vague terminology, especially abstractions, makes readers react adversely:

> It would entail a reasonable and proper evaluative determination to arrive at a conclusive judgment.

If ever it was possible to deluge readers with superfluous words, that game has now been played too often to work. *The New York Times* commented critically: "Topps Chewing Gum finds it difficult to say 'Our products are selling well.' Instead, it declares 'Our established products continue to exhibit consumer acceptance.' "[1] Here is another inundation:

> A reduction in uncertainty is conducive to innovation in the event that it gives the entrepreneur an incremental degree of confidence in planning a program for production purposes.

By contrast, concrete wording quickly tells its own story:

> Raw sewage was being discharged into an open ditch at the rear of the property.

Often, the more words, the less sense. A smoke screen of verbiage hides lack of substance. Such a trick is not newly discovered:

> Words are like leaves, and where they most abound,
> Much fruit of sense beneath is rarely found.[2]

The most hazardous of all word games is subjectivity; again it may be intentional or unintentional. The subjective word (one whose meaning is internal so far as both writer and reader are concerned), like "proper," "adequate," "sufficient," "significant," or "material," depends upon (1) what the author regards as "proper," and so on, and (2) what the reader regards as "proper," and so on. Conspicuous subjectivity is illustrated in the statement that one manager acted "impulsively." Another illustration occurs in the allegation that the "assistant circumvented the requirement."

The objective word (one whose meaning is more stable) is less open to different interpretations. A completely objective term, if there is such a thing, has a commonly understood definition; that is, it denotes rather than connotes.

Both objectivity and subjectivity are likely to be found in one passage:

> Field office efforts to increase exports by providing international trade information and services to United States firms have modestly assisted in achieving export expansion.

"Field office," "export," "trade information," and "United States firms" are objective; subjectivity is apparent in "modestly" and in "expansion." A statement of background data is usually factual and therefore more objective:

> The Program provides revenues to offset operating costs from fees charged to home buyers in the participating countries.

Both categories are useful if recognized for their differing effects.

As a special kind of subjectivity, negative words ("not," "never," "do not," "claim," "allege," and "failed," to name just a few) will antagonize rather than convince if carried too far. Some are obligatory in an audit report. Resistance to excessive negativism blocks results. "Verbal aggression" is what the psychologists label it. Centuries ago, an expert in the art of practical communication noted that: "Men create oppositions which are not; and put them into new terms so fixed as whereas the meaning ought to governeth the term, the term in effect governeth the meaning."[3] Tearing down all negatives is equally self-defeating because accounting does not deal with the best of all possible worlds. The in-between course is to let facts speak for themselves objectively, which many reports do:

> Pricing agencies were permitted during conferences to increase the input into school courses without adequately documenting the basis for doing so.

Subjectivity is not always a losing game; in recommendations and summaries, persuasiveness may be injected by subjective comments, either positive or negative in nature. Convincing, subjective terminology added to the effectiveness of an audit of overseas housing guarantees:

> The relative *affluence* of home buyers plus the availability of mortgage money at *whatever terms* constitutes effective *demand*. The largely domestic origin of labor and materials in economies characterized by high unemployment constitutes *elastic supply*. These conditions suggest a market which would have produced the houses without *infusion* of housing guarantee money.

Wording that suffers, however, from inflation, unconvincing subjectivity, or excessive negativism does not work. Such games may conceal lack of thought, decisiveness, or candor. Straight, plain talk, stripped down to a factual foundation upon which to base opinions, produces the best results in the least amount of space.

Redundancy

Length can be reduced by not repeating the same words and by not restating the same points. Cutting is the easiest way to revise, especially if the report-drafter is the one to do it. If the primary statement of the condition has to be reduced to two lines from four, it is wiser for the person closest to the situation to do it. Wording, rather than content, is what can be eliminated. As Francis Bacon put it centuries ago: "... it is one thing to abbreviate by contracting, another by cutting off."[4]

As a case for "contracting" verbiage versus "cutting off" content, accounting language has habitually included phrases like:

... in the amount of ...

... for the period of ...

... for the months of ...

The meaning would not normally change if they were deleted:

Overdue charges (in the amount) of $3,672 were found.

We audited the performance of the Department for (the months of) July, August, and September.

The accounts receivable were checked for (the period of) March 1 through March 31, 19___.

Dropping even one word takes a straw off the reader's back.

Another kind of redundancy comes from doubling the wordage:

... help alleviate (why not just "alleviate"?)

... homogenized enough (is uniformity a matter of degree?)

... 8:00 A.M. in the morning (when else is A.M.?)

... within a given time frame (why not "within a given time"?)

... past history (when else is "history"?)

The most glaring kind of double take results from adding extra syllables, as in "irregardless," which is thus transformed into a double negative and becomes a contradiction in terms.

A further symptom of superfluity may be described as "pairing," that is, using a pair of words where one would do:

... practical and feasible

If one of the pair is stronger, that is the word to save:

... review and evaluate (if a matter is to be evaluated, it would have to be reviewed)

... reasonable and sound (how could soundness exist without reasonableness?)

Pairing, which reflects a desire to emphasize, is habit-forming. A report which contains one instance is almost sure to have more, at the expense of brevity. Emphasis is weakened, not strengthened, when readers catch onto the game.

Not all words used together are wasted, as, for instance:

... efficiency and effectiveness

... responsibility and authority

... timely and accurate

The intended distinction must be evident at first glance so that there is no stopping to puzzle out the two. Rereading to split hairs is not conducive to brevity. One reviewer in evaluating job performance explained that:

The cashier at the open window experienced apprehension and concern for the functions assigned.

Though the reviewer, interpreting "apprehension and concern" as synonymous and negative, cut one, the writer meant something else. The final draft made the distinction worth two words:

The cashier at the open window felt both fear of and commitment to the functions assigned.

In a variety of small ways, wordiness can be overcome by those who are willing to take the knife to their own drafts. The difference between speaking and writing is worth noting on this point. As an example, articles ("the," "a," and "an") may be dropped from some, but not all, headings:

(The) Unrecognized Obligations

(An) Authorized Staff Level

(A) Prescribed Identification Process

Long quotations can be shortened by replacing irrelevant portions either at the beginning or in the middle with three dots, and at the end with four (the fourth representing the period). Paraphrasing, provided the restating is objective, may make the full quotation expendable.

Omission of "that" is often, but not always, possible, and dropping "that" can save both space and repetitiveness. Omission across the board will make the reader suffer if the connective would have forestalled the misreading possible without "that":

> The Director indicated vulnerable loans in liquidation as a percent of provision for losses would increase.

When the reader reaches "would increase," it becomes necessary to backtrack. Inclusion of "that" after 'indicated" takes a little more space but saves time.

Names of individuals seldom can be cut short. For the sake of formality, before last names the titles "Mr.," "Mrs.," "Miss," and "Ms." (or more specific titles like "Vice-President") customarily precede the initials (or the full first name) in American usage. The widespread adoption in recent years of "Ms." is a sign of the times. "Ms." is a convenient way of addressing women when their marital status is unknown or irrelevant to the situation. Some women like "Ms."; some do not. The essential thing about names is to address individuals as they prefer. The treatment accorded all should be consistent. If all courtesy titles are dispensed with, female as well as male, as some advocate, a new precedent will supplant the old.

Brevity is to be measured in reading time even more than by sheer length. This being the case, "and/or" (another habit-forming device) entails three readings if the total logical purport is analyzed. Its use is validated or invalidated accordingly. In legal context more than in auditing, the triple rereading proves valid. However, writers in general throw in the time-consuming command of "and/or" in an effort to cover all possibilities. In doing so, they cause the phrase to boomerang on one of its three meanings:

> Examples consist of controls added to the computer system to detect and/or prevent error....

Two renditions are logical: The controls can prevent or the controls can detect, but they cannot do both simultaneously, as is implied. If errors are prevented, they will not be there to be detected. Such sweeping use of the legalistic expression is imprecise. The legitimate threefold use appears less often:

> The journal entries are to transfer expenditures and/or revenues.

Though three readings do pay off in this example, the reader might get all three more handily in another way:

> The journal entries are to transfer expenditures or revenues or both.

Among the many other redundancies is the addition of "or not" to "whether":

> We were unable to verify whether or not the number of sales made was supported by invoices.

As soon as an absolute veto is given to such a phrase, another sentence will be found in which the extra words are justified:

> Expenses are recorded on the basis of services performed or goods received whether or not invoices have been received or payments made.

The full sense demands "or not" here, though such an instance is uncommon. Still another chance to cut occurs when the three words "in order to" can be reduced to one: "to."

The form for numbers in sums of money, dates, or series of items offers a chance for greater brevity as well as consistency. The flat rule (write out numbers under one hundred and use figures for one hundred and over) does not take into account consistency in a series. In the many reports where high and low numbers occur together, the figures take less space and stand out on a page. Their use instead of words (disregarding a breakpoint) is increasing. If the numeral is put first in a sentence, the old rule to write it out should be observed to enforce separation from the preceding period. Dollar amounts are expressed by some as "$3 million" or "3 million dollars" instead of "$3,000,000." Whatever way is chosen, it should be uniformly followed.

Dates, often abbreviated "11/3/84," are better treated in formal reports as "November 3, 1984," or still better in military style: "3 November 1984" (to keep the figures apart). The danger of the slashed form (including the computer version of "11/03/84") is that in other countries the same date is written in reverse order as "3/11/84." International distribution of reports makes either the American or the overseas abbreviation ambiguous.

Striking redundancy comes from typing a number twice:

> The twenty-three (23) violations....

This common secretarial practice may have been introduced to ensure accuracy prior to typewriting (and is still advisable for hand-written material). Not only is it wasteful otherwise, but some readers are insulted by the implication that they will not read or remember the number unless it is repeated.

Lack of reading time and interruption of readers' attention are intensifying the demand for conciseness, a demand that one renowned "executive" eloquently expressed during World War II. Winston S. Churchill sent a memorandum to the heads of governmental departments in London on the subject of brevity:

> To do our work we all have to read a mass of papers. Nearly all of them are far too long. . . .

> Let us have an end of such phrases as these: "It is also of importance to bear in mind the following considerations. . . ." or "Consideration should be given to the possibility of carrying into effect. . . ." Most of these woolly phrases are mere padding which can be left out altogether, or replaced by a single word. . . .

> Reports drawn up on the lines I propose may at first seem rough as compared with the flat officialese jargon. But the saving in time will be great. . . . [5]

CLARIFICATION

When asked to name the most desirable qualities in functional communications, respondents may put "brevity" first, but "clarity" runs a close second. Having committed themselves to clear wording, report-writers sometimes practice the opposite, subconsciously if not consciously, by using abstract, trite, subjective terms that may not be familiar. The unavowed intent may be to appear clear but without revealing much. This kind of gamesmanship is dishonest if it serves the writer's interests at the expense of the reader's. Verbosity and vagueness, whether knowingly or unknowingly practiced, subvert the real purpose.

Some word games can undoubtedly be justified, if mutual agreement can be established, but wording should not bury the meaning. Imprecision is usually caused by unintended misuse of words that defeats the best of games. Pitfalls in language are everywhere, but those in audit reports include attributing human characteristics to inhuman objects, employing gender-restrictive pronouns, building up multiple modifiers, misspelling, and injecting foreign expressions.

Finding imprecision

Carelessness in the use of an inexact word may be caught if writers reread their drafts after setting them aside overnight. Careless construction stops readers short:

> Stack samples were collected in a five liter bag.

From "a five liter bag," it is impossible to tell whether all samples were put in one bag or in separate bags of the size indicated. If mere articles like "a" before "bag" cause confusion, prepositions like "at" instead of "with," and "of" instead of "in" make trouble too:

> ... the ease at which one could obtain the desired level.

Other loose combinations produce ludicrous interpretations:

> ... personal factors of trucks. ...

The difference between "compared to" and "compared with" is slight, but the preposition "to" after this verb may imply inequality between the objects being compared. The preposition "with" may not carry this implication.

Another unconscious slip is related to use of the safeguarding qualification in conjunction with "not" and "all":

> All the scheduled appointments were not filled.

Does this mean that no appointments were filled or that some were unfilled? The probable intent was to say:

> Not all the scheduled appointments were filled.

Outright mistakes arise from certain words that sound similar but are not, "accept" and "except" being a case in point. There are many more:

> The responsible officials were appraised of the lack of controls.

"Apprised" (informed) would have made sense, but "appraised" (evaluated) does not.

Other offenders are "affect" and "effect." "Affect" is normally a verb (usually meaning "to influence"), and "effect" is normally a verb or a noun (usually meaning "to bring into existence"). "Affected" is proper here:

> The unbalanced distribution of personnel interfered with the preparation of the stock and *affected* the sales.

The correctness of "affected" can be checked by substituting as a synonym "influenced." If the substitution works, "affected" (and its various forms) is probably correct. The same substitution will not work for "effect":

> Filling requirements by recalling loans could be especially advantageous in order to *effect* quick shipments on high-priority goods.

The synonymous phrase by which to check "effect" is "bring into existence." As a testing device, noninterchangeable substitutes may prove more practical than lexicographic analysis. (There are exceptions, as there are to most things in language.)

Confusion between words that superficially resemble each other but have little resemblance in actuality makes the writer look ridiculous:

> At four sites, 5,114 potentially duplicate outpatient bills valued at about $116,000 were paid without first determining their duplicity.

Figures of speech like metaphors (implied comparisons) are rare in reports. It is hard to get agreement on the exact meaning of figurative language, appealing as it may be:

> The housing guarantee has primed the pump more than $3 million into the region.

Not only is the mental picture of a pump trite, it cannot be sharply focused in its context. Even more unfortunate are mixed metaphors:

> The study was well rounded from every angle.

The pitfalls of imprecision to which wording exposes the writer can only be illustrated, not completely cataloged. No one said it better than Shakespeare: "Suit the action to the word, the word to the action. . . ."[6]

Humanizing the inhuman

On-the-job readers are apt to resist the attribution of animate characteristics to inanimate objects:

> The production plant's dissatisfaction with working conditions was discussed.

The objection is that a production plant cannot feel dissatisfaction, though employees in the plant can. Likewise:

> . . . the review recommends. . . .

> . . . the census states. . . .

> . . . the system evaluates. . . .

In creative writing (as in poetry or prose fiction), such a style is known as "personification" (the representation of a thing as a person) or as the "pathetic fallacy" (attribution of human traits to inanimate objects). In everyday style it is defended by the user who sees the whole in terms of the individuals constituting it (the employees in the plant), but personification is rejected by those who are less familiar with the whole. The problem can easily be resolved by changing:

... the military base is in agreement. ...

to:

... personnel at the military base agree. ...

Implying sex exclusiveness

Professional personnel in the audit field and many other fields, who were once predominantly male, now include many women as writers and readers. For known individuals, the pronouns of masculine gender ("he," "him," "his") as well as the feminine forms ("she," "her," "hers") can be precise designators. In reference to mixed groups, gender-exclusive pronouns are no longer accepted as accurate. For subjective as well as objective reasons, the old habit of using "he" for a male or female is undergoing change.

Influential organizations in public and private fields (federal departments, business corporations, publishers) have set forth sweeping changes. In addition to the unclear pronouns, words like "instructress," "poetess," "chairman," and "man-days" have been banned. Difficult as it is to find nonrestrictive replacements for some long-standing terms (and ridiculous as it is to carry the linguistic revolution too far), the need to do so will mount until discrimination is eradicated in the working world itself as well as in its semantic carry-over. Gendered words are a call to battle for some readers.

The easiest solution for the old use of "he" for both sexes is to switch from the singular to the plural, "they," which does not signify either gender:

The auditors find their work demanding.

The construction "he or she" is obviously contrived and may, in itself, invite the question: Why not "she or he"?

Other possibilities lie in using terms like "staff member," "officer," "investigator," "consultant," "economist," and "accountant." The pronoun "one" is free of gender. As soon as clarification is achieved by ceasing to use the masculine form to refer to both sexes, readers' sensitivities on this issue will subside. Language inevitably becomes the red flag in times of social change. If language keeps pace with the times, current conditions will be reflected accurately on paper.

Combining modifiers

In a report on an agricultural institution, one of the opening sentences contained an ambiguous phrase that was to be repeated later, each time without clarification:

> The credit extended included uncollected beginning farmer loans.

The relationship of "beginning" to the ensuing words is confusing. Is the farmer or the loan beginning? One simple little mark, a hyphen, would have prevented the uncertainty: "uncollected beginning-farmer loans," that is, loans to new farmers.

Because of the complexity of the working world, single modifiers do not always suffice. Not only are the old compounds prominent ("short-term leave," "long-range planning," "year-end inventory"), new and unusual combinations are also coming into play:

> . . . a work-responsibility profile. . . .
>
> . . . December-reported ending checkbook balance. . . .
>
> . . . the artificial-intelligence department. . . .

Authorities do not agree on all uses of the hyphen. The policy is thus up to the writers themselves, who must decide what will be of most assistance for their audience.

Spelling

There is no question as to the psychological distraction of one misspelled word in a business communication. Spelling is not logical; it cannot be based on pronunciation, derivation, or phonetic principles, all of which are contradicted in many established spellings. There is no rhyme or reason to explain why it is necessary to put:

> I before E
> Except after C
> Or when sounded like A
> As in "neighbor" and "weigh."[7]

What makes it so important to spell properly? The answer is that readers come to a halt over a mistake. Their flow of thought is broken, and an opportunity is presented to turn upon the writer for carelessness. The reader's inclination is to say, "I had to struggle to spell correctly, so why shouldn't you?"

If the spelling in a report is not reliable, doubt spreads as to the reliability of the content. Few of the very good writers say that they were born good spellers; they had to learn to live with a dictionary. Every author is expected to do as much out of common courtesy. Wrong spelling is not a first-grade problem; it is a lifelong one.

The most open-minded thinkers remain strict about spelling. Reformers have tried to simplify it, from George Bernard Shaw to writers for *The Chicago Tribune,* but traditions prevail. "Through" is still safer than "thru." Like "tho" for "though," these shortcuts are not formal enough to suit everyone.

There is nothing that a critical reviewer finds more quickly than a slip like:

preceed	for precede
accomodate	for accommodate
counsel	for council (or vice versa)
concensus	for consensus
compliment	for complement (or vice versa)
catagory	for category
heighth	for height
principle	for principal (or vice versa)
supercede	for supersede

In recent years, misspelling has increased in spite of loud protestations. People are spelling the way they hear rather than the way they see. More time is spent listening to words (often carelessly enunciated) than looking at them. The radio, telephone, television, tapes, and loudspeakers contribute to the fallacy of spelling by ear:

inneraction for interaction

asterix for asterisk

beauracrat for bureaucrat

propably for probably

intreguing for intriguing

martial for marital

were for where

weather for whether

whorehouse for warehouse

publically for publicly

cronological for chronological

nitch for niche

repore for rapport

possession for position

quite for quiet

perspective for prospective

enumerable for innumerable

intentially for intentionally

disperse for disburse

introductry for introductory

reconizing for recognizing

behign for behind

curriculm for curriculum

incidently for incidentally

accoutability for accountability

fine for find

probally for probably

osterity for austerity

voracity for veracity

The spelling of words like "traveling" and "controlling," in which a consonant like "l" follows a vowel like "e" or "o," raises questions for many about doubling that consonant. This question is easy to settle. The recommended practice is to double unless the word is accented on the first syllable. In "controlling," the primary stress is not on the first syllable, so the consonant is doubled. In "traveling," the primary stress does fall on the first syllable, so the consonant remains single.

Logical or not, correct spelling remains a status symbol in a literate society. Writers must make their work beyond reproach. Secretaries can help, but the blame for the least oversight comes home to roost with the originator of the report. In view of all that is at stake, use of the dictionary and wordbooks is the only sure means of self-protection.

Introducing foreign words

Borrowing words from Latin, Greek, or other languages was more effective when the schools and colleges required courses in them. The term *ab initio* in a state audit might once have been understood by members of the legislative body to which the report was submitted:

> If the study is made prior to implementation of the program, it may be determined that state funds will not be available to continue the program and that it should be avoided *ab initio*.

It is doubtful today whether most readers would understand "*ab initio*" ("from the beginning") without looking it up.

A particular confusion arises from the use of the Latin abbreviations:

> i.e. (id est), meaning "that is"
>
> e.g. (exempli gratia), meaning "for example"

Though distinct in meaning, these two convenient devices appear indeterminately:

> The matters of record are numerous, i.e., workpapers.

The impression is conveyed by "i.e." that the matters of record consist only of workpapers. Since such a statement is self-contradictory, the author probably meant "for example" and should have written:

> The matters of record are numerous, e.g., workpapers.

Even when the writer knows the translation well enough to be precise, not all readers can be expected to know it. The English equivalents are surer. Besides, use of any foreign wording raises the old possibility of having to underline, an expensive possibility.

Another Latin abbreviation, "etc.," is ordinarily translated correctly ("et cetera," meaning "and other things") but causes another difficulty. It confronts readers with the task of figuring out all the items the writer has in mind but does not bother enumerating. Its effect is questionable except when the listing is self-evident, as the context would make it in this nontypical instance:

> All sixteen accounts named should be numbered from the first to the last—
>
> 1. Purchase of end items
> 2. Supply of spare parts
> Etc.

Provided it is not essential for the reader to conjure up every last detail, the writer can drop the coercive "etc." in favor of "such as" or "including":

> The regulations provide for essentials such as staff qualifications and patients' eligibility.

Of course, "etc." used with "such as" leads to redundancy because "such as" means that only examples are being given.

Certain other borrowed terms are more familiar and therefore better received:

> ad hoc ("for the particular situation")
>
> verbatim ("word for word")
>
> per capita ("by or for each person")
>
> versus (vs.) ("against," "in contrast to")
>
> per ("through," "by means of," "according to," "each")
>
> sic ("thus" useful in quoting respondents' words without change or correction)

Clarity comes in large part from precise wording, which may be undermined in numberless ways. Frequent causes of imprecision are unfamiliar foreign terms, unconnected modifiers, misspelling, offensive pronouns, and unacceptable personification. Detailed though these points are, details make up the whole.

CRITERIA FOR WORDING

As the prime objective of reporting, clarity cannot take second place to brevity. Being short is useless if the content is ambiguous. Over-compression is not real brevity. In reports that are intended to be permanent, precise, and properly pinpointed in distribution, the wording has to be both clear and brief.

To achieve the double goal, criteria for word selection can be set up in advance of drafting. Recurrent errors, if anticipated, can be prevented. Regarding jargon (technical language), there are more weak points than strong. When simple synonyms cannot be found, definitions are the solution. Though audits are performed within "walled communities," few of the reports are surrounded by any such protective barriers. Overstandardization results in a trite, tedious, uncommunicative style. But, just as with a limited amount of specialized wording, some codification is part of professionalism.

Like water in a glass, wording seeks its own level. Starting with a modern dictionary, writers can narrow down their choice from among the thousands of words by observing professional requirements. They will adapt their style to the new demands of operational coverage without abandoning entirely the traditions of formality. Above all, the end product (the report) must show in condensed, convincing, clarified language those conditions which make correction imperative.

NOTES

[1] *The New York Times,* Mar. 26, 1975. © 1975 by The New York Times Company. Reprinted by permission.

[2] Alexander Pope, "Essay on Criticism," in *The Complete Works of Alexander Pope,* Houghton Mifflin Company, Boston, 1903, p. 71.

[3] C. S. Northrup (ed.), *The Essays of Francis Bacon,* Houghton Mifflin Company, Boston, 1908, p. 13.

[4] Ibid, p. 78.

[5] S. W. Roskill, *The Art of Leadership,* William Collins Sons & Co., Ltd., London, 1964, p. 119.

[6] William Shakespeare, *Hamlet,* Act II, Scene 2, in William Allen Neilsen (ed.), *The Complete Works of William Shakespeare,* Houghton Mifflin Company, Boston, 1906, p. 913.

[7] Note some exceptions, including "weird," "foreigner," "either," "neither," "leisure," and "height."

3 Streamlining sentences

Although vocabulary is a matter that concerns report-writers, sentence construction raises even more questions. The most challenging task in logical style is composing a clear, explicit sentence. What appears to be a simple act of putting together a subject (that is, naming the topic) and a predicate (that is, giving the main action about that topic) opens up unsuspected complications. The sentence, as the vehicle for a complete thought, travels a course beset with roadblocks; the longer the road, the likelier the vehicle is to encounter obstructions.

Length involves not only more reading time but also the probability of blocked meaning. The dimensions of a unit of thought need to be judged not only by the space the thought occupies but by the time required to grasp the thought. To follow the idea accurately, the reader depends upon the writer's observance of certain conventions, for communication depends upon a two-way system of output and intake.

The way to accelerate the reading and the writing of audit material is to build units that are both short and accurate. This results in understandability and acceptability. Many reports contain certain errors that defeat the purpose of reporting. These mistakes, though limited to about a half dozen, are recurrent and they are ruinous.

A whole series of short, correct sentences is not all that it takes to make material readable and convincing. Monotony causes loss of attention. Sentences may be precise without being effective. What is then lacking is a versatility of pattern, that extra quality which keeps the thought process moving. Over and above the kinds of sentences classified in the schoolroom, writers on the job instinctively develop their own ways of changing pace.

MATTERS OF DIMENSION

Easy as it is to advocate reducing length and simplifying structure, thoughts that are neither short nor simple have to be conveyed. Weaving in qualifications, making reservations, and restricting implications (all of which have to be done) add to the number of words between the capital letter and the period. Then it is that the exact sense hangs upon the bare bones of grammar. Accurate interpretation depends upon traditional construction. As the number of words accumulates, the grammatical essentials become demonstrably harder to preserve.

Overloading

To turn talk into print requires the retention of the free flow heard in conversation, reinforced by written conventions. At the same time, the risk of overloading any one sentence has to be kept in mind. Spoken sentences are carried successfully by intonation of voice, by tempo, and by gesture. Once reduced to print, they need to be shortened for quick intake.

Most long sentences actually are not run-on sentences, though these are certainly faulty and overburdened. The run-on consists of two (or more) sentences without a connecting word (a conjunction) or a semicolon:

> We estimated 6 hours to establish burden rates, the result proved insufficient.

The comma should be a period. Overloading more typically comes from crowding too many ideas together. Readers stagger from the lack of opportunity to catch a breath.

Measuring

Not all ordinary matters of business can be stated simply and memorably in short units. A sentence may become so long that the writer loses the way and encounters roadblocks. Even an accurately constructed thought may be too long for easy grasp. Whether correct or incorrect, the unit becomes overloaded.

In everyday dealings some topics demand elaboration and are

neither definitive nor absolute, and so a stretch-out commences from a simple start:

In most cases, drugs were labeled.

Omission of the initial modifying words, "In most cases," would lead to imprecision, although they do increase the length. Some might then add another phrase and another modifier:

In most cases, *but not in all*, drugs were *properly* labeled.

This sentence, with its greater emphasis and exactitude, is still a quick, comprehensible one consisting of only eleven words, well below the actual average found in reports.

Most writers who are reporting on important affairs in American business and government average approximately twenty-two words per sentence. The figure is not necessarily good or bad. It is simply a real count, reflecting an average (derived during the last decade) of words per sentence in the style of supervisory personnel who have participated in hundreds of on-the-job seminars on report-writing. The figure, though given as being neither right nor wrong, is a proven one, representing the average length produced under the pressure of content and responsibility. Just as a thermometer responds to temperature, verbiage rises or falls according to the working environment.

As the burden of facts and conclusions intensifies, the sentence may soften and expand. The number of words is actually only one measure of readability. The number of ideas has more to do with extent, so that the ideas are variously packaged. A mere phrase (that is, a group of words without its own subject and predicate, such as that italicized) may provide sufficient modification:

Service was provided *within the allotted time*.

In the interests of further factuality, a clause may be added (that is, a group of words containing its own subject and predicate):

Service was provided within the allotted time *if the mechanics were available.*

Such a clause cannot stand alone, since it is dependent on the rest of the sentence for its meaning (a dependent clause). Another kind of addition is a group of words not only containing its own subject and predicate but also capable of standing alone (that is, an independent clause):

Service was provided within the allotted time if the mechanics were available, and *the results were found to be satisfactory.*

The reader has now been given a larger point as amplified by one phrase, one dependent clause, and one independent clause; seven words have grown to twenty in order to do the job. To make the reader see some connection between the first and the second parts of the thought, the writer coupled them by using "and" instead of a period.

Coupling

Grammatically, the coupled sentence is not incorrect. Its increased extent, nevertheless, imposes upon the reader the task of keeping in mind everything from beginning to end. Coupling by "and" is a habit of many writers:

> We made the appropriate adjustments to eliminate costs attributed to maintenance of privately owned equipment, *and* for other costs omitted from the study, *and* determined that the cost of in-house operation actually was $8,251 more than the cost would be if maintenance services were obtained by contract.

Replacing the coupler ("and") before "determined" by a period and starting with a new sentence, if the thoughts do not have to be read together, quickens the pace. Use of more than one "and" causes uncertainty as well as delay because different degrees of separation are intended. In the finding quoted, the first "and" indicates a lesser break than the second, which is where the two major ideas are coupled. The more ideas that have to be read in combination, the more time the reader must spend.

At times in functional material, the interlocking of two or more thoughts may have to be shown without permitting their separation by the full stop (the period). Coupling, in such a case, may not be strong enough to convey the distinctive relationship. A more significant connective may give the reader greater help than the weak equating as shown by "and":

> We reviewed repair times reported on the maintenance request register *and* found that times reported were not in agreement with the report on earned hours.

Instead of equating the two thoughts, the first one can be subordinated, and emphasis thrown onto the second (and more important) one:

> When we reviewed repair times reported on the maintenance request register, we found that times reported were not in agreement with the report on earned hours.

The idea of chronology has here replaced the idea of equating. Cause and effect is another valuable relationship if it is not desirable to break thoughts apart:

> Budget restraints were imposed; therefore services were curtailed.

"Therefore" says much more than "and" would have signified cause. Subordination, chronology, and cause and effect are only a few of the signals that are stronger than coupling.

Overloaded sentences are those which are allowed to run wild as to the number of words, the combination of ideas, or the complexity of structure. By cutting the units down to size, writers can protect themselves against the typical roadblocks. Grammatical breakdown shows a high correlation with sentence length.

STRUCTURAL ACCURACY

Out of all the historical rules for accurate construction, functionally minded communicators have to find and follow those which are indispensable to their needs. In determining which rules these are, allowance has to be made for the varying levels of individuals' experience and of organizations' aspirations. Perfection, or near perfection, requires the application of a host of historical rules, some of which may not be necessarily relevant to contemporary reporting. As the pressure for fast issuance of material mounts, corners have to be cut.

Perfectionism

One restriction on the letter-perfect, rule-book approach is the lack of time available for writing. Another variable is the fact that, as the times change, so does usage of the language. At what point does the enforcement of rules reach the point of diminishing returns?

For instance, is it "wrong" to split infinitives? That very phrase strikes terror from grammar school days; yet most readers are not bothered by a statement like this:

> The survey was designed to completely search the records.

The infinitive (that is, the verb "search" preceded by "to") is certainly split by the modifier ("completely") inserted in the middle. Split infinitives are found in the books of well-known authors, in reputable periodicals, and on the lips of professional speakers. The taboo against splitting infinitives may have arisen from awkward instances:

> Such a terminal is required to completely and promptly program the computer.

The phrase "to completely and promptly program" is a doubly split infinitive and is extremely awkward. If writers are going to concern themselves with such rules as that concerning the split infinitive, they should do so on the basis of awkwardness, not merely because an infinitive has been split. There are sentences in which splitting may actually be necessary to avoid the wrong meaning. For instance, how could the precise point be preserved here without splitting the infinitive?

A review is essential to adequately guide personnel involved in purchasing duties.

What other principles might be scratched in the name of good sense? Some say that the old distinction between "shall" and "will" has vanished. In this distinction, tense, person, and number are all involved, requiring intricate explanation of voluntary and involuntary future:

Person	Voluntary future	Involuntary future
First person: I (We)	...shall go.	...will go.
Second person: You	...will go.	...shall go.
Third person: He, She, It (They)	...will go.	...shall go.

Except in dealing with legal, contractual material or specifications, few writers have the time or need to keep the distinction alive.

Then there are other distinctions, like that once enforced between "can" and "may," which are now no longer universally respected. Commonly, the expression "due to" is substituted for "because of." The words "while" and "since" are no longer used solely in connection with time, although some do not approve of such changes.

What about ending a sentence with a preposition? In talking, it is common to do so, and in writing, there are occasions when a word like "by," "for," or "with" seems best as the last one:

The daily receipts are regularly accounted for.

Usually, it is possible to get around ending a sentence with a preposition and thereby avoid offending some readers. Behind the rule about the preposition may lie the fact that it is not normally the kind of word worth emphasizing. Whatever stands last should not be a weak word, as it is here:

It proved possible to locate the individuals we wished to consult with.

When the principle of emphasis is at stake, revision is worthwhile so that the part of speech lives up to its name (literally, "pre-positioned"):

> It proved possible to locate the individuals with whom we wished to consult.

Again, it is not the rule so much as a logical or psychological principle (emphasis) that determines the validity of usage.

Common denominators

Although writers and co-writers, including editorial reviewers, set their own sights, possibly going beyond those imperfections to which all are prone, loss of meaning comes from six roadblocks that have to be surmounted by all who do not wish to be ambiguous. The limited number of these common problems should be reassuring to those who, not being specialists in English, worry about the overbearing problem of "grammar."

Of course, the hand-me-down "rules" for being "right" are countless, but not all of them are crucial. Nor are all applicable in up-to-date usage. Language changes with the times. The few "imperatives" that do apply can be confined to (1) those which control clarity and, within that category, (2) those which are violated most frequently.

Standards of logic and psychology underlie the rules of grammar which cannot be ignored. For practical purposes, it is possible to identify those most likely to render a thought overburdened, incomplete, or unclear. Once that practical goal has been attained, writers or their reviewers may, if their time permits, go further in pushing improvement toward perfection. But it was Churchill who was credited with the remark that there is another way to spell "perfection," and that is "paralysis." Different organizations seek different levels of correctness.

The most commonly encountered obstructions that interfere with clarity and acceptability, though few in number, are disastrous in their consequences:

Ambiguous pronouns

Dangling participles

Disagreement in number

Misplaced modifiers

Nonparallelism

Pyramiding.

These are by no means the only violations that crop up in report-writing, but their elimination will provide an insurance policy of basic clarity.

Valid grammar is explainable in terms of reason and precedent; to a certain extent, therefore, the jargon of grammar (syntactical terminology) does not have to be the starting point.

Ambiguous pronouns.   As the first example of roadblocks related to the sentence unit, words that stand for other words (pronouns) require caution. Pronouns carry with them both advantages and disadvantages. "This" is the most conspicuous in functional usage. As a replacement for something specific that has previously been identified, "this" forestalls repetition of the same word and is shorter:

> We visited the manufacturing *plant. This* is located in. . . .

The reference (called the antecedent) of the replacement word ("this") is unmistakable ("plant"), and repetition has been avoided. It is unusual to make such simple statements; more often "this" seems to refer back to a whole concept:

> These weaknesses increase the possibility of defalcation or error because control over cash receipts is neither established nor maintained. *This* is in need of immediate correction.

Does "this" stand for the weaknesses, the increase, the possibility, the defalcation, the errors, the lack of control, or the failure to maintain control? The writer, at the time, undoubtedly knew, but the reader, faced with a guessing game, is inclined to bow out. Vague, all-inclusive backward references of such substitute words ("it," "these," "those," "which," "they," "them," "theirs," and others) are open to misinterpretation:

> XYZ should find out if the articles of unknown ownership and those belonging to headquarters are needed, and those not needed should be disposed of. Transferred personnel should be notified that storage has custody of the articles. If the owners do not take action to recover their articles, they should be disposed of.

" . . . they"? Frankly, is XYZ supposed to dispose of owners?

Unclear use of replacement words (literally, "pro-nouns") is, strange to say, characteristic of senior personnel:

> Equipment was shipped to the Northeast office under the terms of the contract, *which* caused a severe shortage in the Midwest region.

Does "which" stand for "contract" (its nearest and likeliest reference point) or for the act of shipping to a particular office? The writer's very familiarity with the situation is what causes the problem. The frequency of the ambiguous pronoun is attributable not so much to ignorance of grammar as to a situational symptom. Being too close to the subject led one operational auditor into this forest of pronouns:

> We also wanted to determine whether managers' orders were following the instruction from the directors wherein *they* stated that if services and supplies *which* had not been requested could not be rectified within the time indicated in *it, it* should not be carried out.

Does "they" take the place of "managers" or "directors"? Does "which" take the place of "supplies" or "services and supplies"? Does the first "it" take the place of "instruction"? Does the second "it" take the place of "instruction" or the act of requesting or of rendering services and supplies?

The solution lies in dividing sentences containing such uncertainties, or in adding a substantive word after such terms as "this," "these," or "those." Division of the foregoing sentence would resolve its mysteries:

> We also wanted to determine whether managers' orders were following the instructions from the directors. The instructions stated that, if services and supplies had not been requested, neither might be rectified within the time indicated by the directors. In that case, the supplies and services should not be carried out.

A substantive addition, indicated in parentheses, is also a solution:

> In twelve of twenty-four delinquencies in our sample of contracts, the procuring official was not notified in a timely manner. These (failures) were due mainly to the clerks' not determining the status of the contract prior to the delivery dates.

Repetition of the same word, though sometimes excessive, is safer than vagueness:

> Another problem found in accounts receivable involves the combining of related but separate corporate *customers* on one total on the accounts receivable listing. These *customers* maintain separate sets of books.

The best-informed report-writers are the ones who need to exercise the greatest care in clarifying their use of replacement words.

Dangling participles.   A word indicating action (a verb in one of its various forms) needs to be accompanied by the doer of the action. When the verb is the main one, there is usually no difficulty:

> We *recommend* three procedures. . . .

When other actions are indicated in a subordinate way in a sentence, the doer should also be clear, either by being named or by being unmistakably implied. One frequent form of the verb in which subordinate action is expressed ends in "-ing" (the present participle):

> We recommend three procedures, *knowing* the difficulty that exists.

"Knowing" is tied into the sentence accurately because it is clear who knows: "We." Less clear, in fact very vague, would have been the statement:

> Knowing the difficulty that exists, three procedures are recommended.

Now it is not apparent who knows the difficulty; certainly it is not the "three procedures." No doer of that action has been mentioned. The dangling participle is the problem: a piece of the action that cannot be traced by the reader to anyone or anything. The action dangles free and unclear, as happens doubly in the second of these two sentences:

> The subscriber to health insurance has no idea of what specific charges are submitted by the doctor or their dollar amount. By *notifying* the subscriber, internal control will be strengthened, thus *ensuring* that benefits are paid only for actual medical services received.

Who is doing the "notifying"? Who is doing the "ensuring"? Dangling participles are a danger because they create imprecision:

> We found a typewriter listed as being on hand without any serial number given for it. *Lacking* the only unique item of identity, ownership of the typewriter would be hard to establish.

In less strict usage, some grammarians feel an implied source of the action may be sufficient:

> *Assuming* the reports are accurate, the caseworkers were satisfactorily screened.

It is, of course, the writer who is "assuming," not the caseworkers. "Necessitating," "regarding," "requiring," and "estimating" are common danglers that may not interfere with clarity. Once the rule is waived, however, writers may ignore it when they cannot afford to do so: In the instance of the typewriter, who or what is "lacking"? Certainly it is the "typewriter" and not the "ownership," as the structure implies. The only writers who should allow themselves deviation are those who have reviewed the rule, appreciate the reason for it, and then make a calculated decision that the dangling participle will not be subject to criticism.

Disagreement in number.   Of incredible frequency is the third road-block to smooth reading. By some quirk, words that are singular are treated as plural within one and the same sentence. The error is so apparent that writers themselves are surprised when it is pointed out to them; most remember from their schooldays that a singular subject takes a singular verb, a plural subject takes a plural verb, a singular noun takes a singular pronoun, and a plural noun takes a plural pronoun. Why does the mismatch happen, as in this quotation?

> We found six areas regarding incentive contracting which, we believe, in current production of the quality desired for successful use, *requires* improvement through management's attention.

The verb "requires" is singular in form (one area "requires"), but its subject is "areas," a plural (two or more areas "require").
 A singular pronoun is likewise incorrect when the noun for which it stands (the antecedent) is plural:

> Comprehensive studies were made of 160 delayed discharges from one institution, *which represents* all such discharges.

Although it obviously stands for a plural ("discharges"), "which" has become incorrectly a singular (as "represents" shows) because of its proximity to "institution," for which the pronoun does not stand.
 Disagreement in number catches the reader's eye as a mark of illiteracy. In all probability it occurs so often because of sentence length rather than ignorance of the rule. Language being a form of the writer's behavior, pressure of content may lead to overloading the vehicle. By the time the author has finally reached the verb, its exact subject has been forgotten. In moving rapidly, the pencil accommodates itself to the nearer source (a singular, "use" or "incentive contracting" in the first extract given) rather than to the actual subject. Even within a smaller compass the same slip may happen:

> Our audit in past years *have* not disclosed significant defects.

"Have" sounds right with "years" (a plural verb standing next to a plural noun) but is not in accord with the true subject, "audit."
 A special dilemma relates to nouns that are singular in form but

plural in meaning, to the user at least. In grammatical jargon these are called "collective nouns," and various rule books say that collectives may be treated as singular or plural. Whenever language offers an option, the writer is faced with making a decision. The policy should not permit inconsistency:

> The branch met their sales objective in March. . . .

"Branch" is a noun singular in form and apparently plural in concept thus far (because of the pronoun "their"). Yet the sentence does not end as it begins:

> The branch met their sales objective in March, but for April that branch is under objective.

The writer changed horses in midstream; "is" is a singular verb.

Each organization develops its own set of collectives. In industry, "company," "firm," "department," "plant," and "staff" are favorites. In government, "agency," "division," "unit," and "activity" are among the many. Auditors, when asked whether they prefer to treat such terms as singular or plural, invariably answer, "Singular." Theoretically, logic supports such a response; each of the collectives named could also have a genuine plural ("companies," "firms," "departments," "divisions," "plants," "staffs," "agencies," "units," "activities"). If the singular of a collective has been given plural treatment in the verb or pronoun, there is no place to go when the real plural has to be expressed:

> The branch met *their* sales objective in March, but for April all the branches *are* under objective.

No differentiation is left for "all the branches."

In actual practice, subconscious use of a plural verb or pronoun in relation to the collective is growing, regardless of the theoretical testimony in favor of the singular:

> The supply function maintained *their* inventory.

"Function" is thought of by the author as a composite group of individuals. The closer the report-writer is to the collective subject under discussion, the more probable it is that the subject will be viewed as the people composing it rather than as a singular entity. In the same report as that just quoted, the reporter later became inconsistent:

> Although the supply function *was* keeping up *their* stocks, *they* had an unrecorded excess.

"Was" makes "function" singular, while "their" and "they" go back to the earlier plural implication of the individuals responsible for the function.

Three words in most report-writers' vocabulary get mixed treatment: "data," "media," and "criteria."

By derivation all are plural; by daily usage they are being treated as singular. Grammarians and logicians shudder to read:

The data *is* on file.

The media *does* not represent findings fully.

The criteria *is* contained in the Regulation.

The Latin singular of the first word is "datum." Surveyors still refer to a "datum line," though the Latin plural ("data") is seen more often and is seen as a singular. The Latin singular of the second word is "medium," but, as one concept, "media" is increasingly used in the singular. The Greek singular of the third word is "criterion," although the concept of "criteria" as a collective body of standards is leading some to use a singular verb or pronoun with it.

Logic has something to lose from this casual, unconscious usage. The writer who treats an original plural as singular has lost the original plural. The next phase, even more unacceptable to grammatically minded readers, is to create new plurals ("datas"? "medias"? "criterias"?). For precise meaning, preservation of forms historically rooted is the safer way in traditional style.

Disagreement in number when collectives are not the complicating factor will automatically right itself if sentences are held down in length. With collectives, a conscious decision between singular and plural has to be made for the sake of consistency. Commonly accepted usage will determine the plurality or singularity of words that are in transit. Smooth sound is important.

Misplaced modifiers.   Seldom do reports contain flat, all-out statements without the necessity of building in qualifications. Sometimes "only," if inserted as an example of a one-word modifier, can be moved around like a checker on a checkerboard:

The auditors told their assistants to take the records on the day specified.

If the modifier "only" is put before the first word in the sentence or after the last, there is a change in meaning. "Only" can also be put between any two words in this sentence, with a different result each time.

Safeguarding of content by modifying words or, more typically, by modifying groups of words may be crucial. Accuracy by means of modification puts pressure on the sentence. In the first place, modifiers naturally lengthen it; and in the second place, they complicate it.

The reader's burden might have been lightened if the first ten words that follow could have ended with a period, but accuracy might have been impaired:

> *It has been our objective to review the audit work* performed by the internal audit staff in order to attempt to establish the degree of assurance that can be placed on the account data system, to the extent that it completely and reliably processes data based on the testing method employed.

The words that come after "performed" are for the sake of limiting or defining the scope of the review. The result is fifty-one words, all of which, when placed in one unit, must be carried in the reader's mind as being interdependent. Here, as with other complexities in structure, the simplest solution would be to find a reasonable stopping place and then to start over:

> It has been our objective to review the audit work performed by the internal audit staff. Our attempt was to establish the degree of assurance that can be placed on the account data system insofar as the system completely and reliably processes data based on the testing method employed.

The second sentence (itself the one that has been carved out of the original version) seems incapable of subdivision lest the limitation on the degree of assurance sought be initially disregarded. In such sentences as the second one in the revised example, the important thing is to place the inseparable modifying phrase or phrases so that they cannot be misrelated. Modifiers are supposed to stand directly adjacent to the words to which they must be applied. Readers, however, read not by the rule book but by the first impression, which should be unmistakable.

Ambiguously placed modifiers most often stand at the end of sentences. The trouble is that the qualifying point comes into play too late:

> In addition to these local and long-haul communications services, the control function is performed by the communication activity *where applicable.*

Is "the control function" the element referred to by the words "where applicable," or is it "the communication activity" that is being described?

The overused words "based on" are another frequent cause of misrelationship:

The demonstration project provides laboratory staff with the option to contract the work or to accomplish it in-house, by adding personnel rather than contractor services *based on a judgment as to how the task can most quickly be performed.*

Are the "services" to be "based . . . "? More probably, the option is to be decided on the basis of a judgment as to how the task can most quickly be performed. "Based on" has become almost idiomatic (that is, peculiar but accepted) in usage because of its frequency in functional communication. At the very least, it should be more closely tied into the sentence than it is in the one given.

Because misplaced modifiers permit more than one possible reading and because modification is indispensable to the safeguarding of meaning, this roadblock has to be removed. Ludicrous interpretations are often unconsciously permitted by loosely related wording:

We weighed all leftover food together with dining-room personnel.

It does not take a long sentence to open up a double meaning.

Nonparallelism. Parallelism means saying similar things in a similar way. The stating of recommendations offers a good illustration:

Recommendations:
  1. *Prepare* a list of all incoming cash receipts at the time the mail is opened.
  2. *Stamp* all incoming checks "For Deposit Only."

Two comparable steps (preparing a list and stamping the mail) have been recommended in the same kind of structure, the imperative form of the verb, which is a favorite for recommendations. As another parallel form, the handle, "We recommend" is built in:

We recommend that:
  a. Prior approval be secured for all overtime.
  b. Employees be supervised more efficiently for their productivity.

For the sake of economy any word that goes with each item ("that" in the example) belongs in the handle and should not be repeated each time.

Parallelism is a speedup device enabling readers to proceed without breaking stride, as to either content or construction. Reading parallel items is like running up a flight of steps without tripping, which can be done only if each tread is the same height.

Nonparallelism causes not only a pause but sometimes a downfall, as in this passage:

> It is necessary to define criteria for determining potential management capability:
>
> 1. When hiring new people is done
> 2. Early in the individual's career.

The reader who is used to encountering enumerated listings expects these items to have consistency, and these do not conform structurally, one being a dependent clause and the other a phrase.

The violation of the readers' conditioned expectations occurs whether nonparallelism appears in recommendations, in listings, or in headings:

> Personnel Practices
>
> Controlling Paychecks
>
> For Management Jurisdiction

Either of the last two headings could be revised to fit the first for structural uniformity, if the assumption is that the content under each heading is, as it should be under headings at the same level, comparable in importance:

> Personnel Practices
>
> Payroll Controls
>
> Management Jurisdiction

Now there is at least structural smoothness. A set of proper headings is needed in any outline format. These are parallel:

> *Items Processed Incorrectly*
>
> I. Reasons:
>   A. Manual decision inaccurate
>   B. Computer decision inaccessible
>
> II. Solutions:
>   A. Correction of manual decision
>   B. Accessibility of computer decision

The reader can follow such an outline without hesitating.

Within a conventional sentence, parallelism provides uninterrupted flow when used with items in a series:

> Employees were observed during working hours *playing cards, washing their autos,* and *doing personal shopping.*

The three criticisms are separate but similar, and each is introduced as an ongoing action (expressed in the "-ing" participle). The opposite is true in another series in which four dissimilar items that are dissimilar in structure slow up rather than expedite the reading process:

> Since *planning, counseling, drug prescriptions,* or *making emergency calls* may be legitimate psychiatric claims, more information is needed in the forms as filed.

Nonparallelism in a more complicated series can be even more frustrating:

> Of the sixty-nine cases we reviewed, *two were not recorded on the register, the cancellation of one was not on the registration,* and *for fifteen the register was not annotated to reflect the issuance of the requisite form.*

The solution in such diffused coverage might be to abandon the attempt at parallelism in favor of separate sentences, thus not setting up a situation with an implicit promise of "like following like."

As a device which permits more than one thing to be said about the handle, parallelism is valuable. The several things that are to be said must be attachable to the one group of words that picks up those several things by the same kind of grooving (structure).

Nonparallelism is a circuit breaker; it stops the current from flowing. It is sometimes employed intentionally in literary style, and the effect is one of shock, as in the titles of two chapters of John Hersey's report *Hiroshima:*

> Details Are Being Investigated (a complete sentence)
>
> Panic Grass and Feverfew (a compound phrase)

Shock, which was Hersey's underlying intent throughout his book, is not normally the communicator's intent, so far as the language is concerned.

In recommendations, enumerations, headings, outlines, series, and (another essential place) procedures, parallelism keeps readers on the track. Nonparallelism leads to derailing.

Pyramiding. Unlike the other recurrent writing problems, that of pyramiding cannot be solved by reviewing lessons learned in grammar school. In fact, this phenomenon scarcely existed when many of today's report-writers were in the schoolroom.

Pyramiding consists of a pileup of nouns (name words) modifying one another, sometimes with a few descriptive words (adjectives) thrown in:

> The *issue price* of a pound of rolls was the same as the *white bread pound price.*

Pyramiding is an outgrowth of the complexity of contemporary affairs. It is also the result of compression; the normal connecting prepositions are simply dropped. When the pileup gives rise to ambiguity, the writer's purpose is defeated:

> A *complete power plant definition* is needed by the operating crew.

The pyramid's peak is "definition." Of the four words piled up, only the first is traditionally a modifier (the adjective "complete"). The others are nouns. An adjective modifies a noun, and so the question is: Which noun? What is "complete"? Does the crew need:

> A definition of a plant with complete power?
>
> A definition of power in a complete plant?
>
> A complete definition of a power plant?

Even readers who have forgotten parts of speech instinctively expect "complete" to be related to some of the other three words; they do not want to sort out all the possibilities for themselves and end up being uncertain.

The reason for the heightening of pyramids, which is part of the phenomenon, lies in the unfolding specializations in modern business, requiring more and more modification. The supply of conventional adjectives having been exhausted, nouns are being thrown into the breach. Many of the instances originate as headings, where the jamming is induced by lack of space. Once the pyramided heading has been created, it moves over into the sentences that follow.

Some of the pyramiding will not cause trouble. Two layers (one noun on top of another) are not a problem: "audit team," "case load," "sample selection." Such modest conversion of parts of speech has long been taken for granted. Some are even written as one word: "railroad," "lamplight," "wallboard."

The danger lies in an unconscious building up of the pile of unconventionally related words. Writers teach themselves new combinations, beginning with a low level like "record maintenance." Soon that activity turns into a system: "records maintenance system" (still only three nouns together). Next comes a real modifier (an adjective), and ambiguity has set in:

Auditors recommend the consolidation of *current records maintenance systems* to accommodate this directive.

If the recommendation is adopted, the "in-group" will before long be referring to:

... current records maintenance systems consolidation.

What is "current"? Records? Maintenance? Systems? Consolidation? Perhaps the recommender meant all items to be taken together as one concept, but not all readers will have the same expectation.

Nouns used as adjectives are no problem if their relationship to one another is clear. Authentic adjectives along with a pileup of nouns will constitute a problem if the adjectives are capable of being tied to different words. Inasmuch as a certain amount of this kind of construction is inevitable in light of today's needs for specification, compromise between the new and the old usage will help straighten matters out.

The compromises required by pyramids may consist of:

Lowering the height by dropping a word or words that are unnecessary

Dividing one high pyramid into two or more lower ones

Taking the peak off the pyramid and moving it to the beginning

Using initial capital letters for the major words, thus indicating that an official caption is being copied exactly with no alteration

Restricting the usage to the heading level

Limiting use of pyramids to those occasions when the normal grammar will not work

Inserting an apostrophe with "s" to turn a noun used as an adjective into a possessive

Hyphenating two words that should be read as one within the group

Enclosing the whole in quotation marks to signal its unusualness

Rearranging the piled-up words with the normal prepositions.

Unlike the other roadblocks in sentence construction (such as the ambiguous pronoun, the dangling participle, disagreement in number, the misplaced modifier, and nonparallelism), pyramiding is a variant that may at times be accepted. Like the other roadblocks, it cannot be accepted if it interferes with accuracy of meaning.

By removing these six common defects from functional writing, most writers will have an insurance policy of basic clarity. By going beyond these causes of ambiguity and meeting such preferences (or even prejudices) as particular reviewers or readers are known to possess, writers may add psychological acceptability to logical impact.

DIVERSITY OR MONOTONY

To eliminate monotony from reading matter means going one step farther than mere correctness and clarity. Variety of sentence pattern helps maintain the reader's interest. Sameness of any aspect of style, in structure as in vocabulary, not only lulls the reader but suggests a limited capacity on the part of the communicator. Just as triteness in vocabulary is a disaffecting quality, so is a string of simple sentences.

Conversation, whether in casual interchange or serious discussion, automatically calls forth questions, exclamations, directions, and declarations. No less a writer than Robert Frost explained the point this way:

> ... there are moments when we actually touch in talk what the best writing can only come near. The curse of our book language is not so much that it keeps forever to the same set phrases ... but that it sounds forever with the same reading tones.[1]

The basis of real communication is give-and-take. In formal writing, the opportunity for that is curtailed.

Classifications

Written reports on operational audits are more restricted than entrance and exit conferences in the kinds of sentences that are used. Not all the types taught in the classroom are normally brought into play, so monotony is a real hazard. As soon as writers try to cut down sentence length, one result may be short, choppy units. The choice between long, varied sentences and short, monotonous ones is not a necessary dilemma. Even within the restricted scope that is usable in reports, a varied pattern can be developed if all options are considered. Among the recognized options, limitations can then be consciously regarded or disregarded.

Exclamatory sentences, being emotionally charged, are seldom useful. They do not convey the sense of careful, deliberate forethought. For the few times when such "outcries" are noted, the authors seem to have consciously invoked the technique of shock. The exclamation mark should, in those rare cases, be properly affixed for full value.

The question is almost as rare as the exclamation, though raising questions could be more effectively employed. An interrogative involves the reader in the response mechanism. If the desired answer is forthcoming from the reader's own mind, the writer has, for the moment anyway, won concurrence on the point. The successful question draws out the obvious conclusion even before the writer has to insist upon it. The posture of argument is not adopted. Readers accept more willingly the answers they give in their own minds than those imposed upon them.

Even before the response stage is reached, interest and curiosity may be aroused, as happened near the beginning of a report on a nutrition program abroad:

The findings deal with five basic questions:

1. Can the nutrition program be effectively managed on an ad hoc basis?
2. Has the nutrition program stimulated progress?
3. Has the nutrition program encouraged the development of local cooperation?
4. Are the results of the nutrition program worth the dollar drain?
5. Will low-cost, long-term loans for the nutrition program work in countries with high rates of inflation?

The report not only began by raising the issues but actually ended by using a question as its last sentence, the author feeling sufficiently confident that the correlation of convincing facts would by that time elicit only the answer desired ("yes"):

The nutrition program has attempted to transplant the tradition of long-term loans into economies that had not generated such a tradition on their own. Had these economies been able to support the institution of long-term loans, would it not have been born of natural economic forces?

Such risk-taking style is not ordinary. Auditors hesitate to pose questions, feeling they are supposed to know all the answers. Nobody does. Asking the right question may get directly to the heart of the matter. If the risk is to be taken, two cautions are worth noting. The first is to use phrasing that will not invite the "wrong" answer. The reader must be led to the position where the reaction will be what the writer believes to be necessary. The second caution is to nail down that answer at once, as a mutual agreement henceforth. Author and reader must arrive at the conclusion almost simultaneously, thus establishing a meeting of the minds. A well-designed question deserves to be followed up by the alert signal of the question mark, not swallowed up by a period with the result that the psychological advantage is lost.

Apart from the reports themselves, the interrogative may appear generally in audit guides where workplans are being set forth. Here, a series of questions requiring investigation within the scope of the review is a convenience for those assigned to the field and a protection for the auditor-in-charge.

Apart from exclamations and questions, commands (that is, sentences containing imperative verbs) are frequently used in stating recommendations. The action implied is quick and definite:

Recommendations for:

The Governor

Set new rate structures.

Require collections.

The Commissioner

Submit proposed rates.

Prepare collection procedures.

More and more, the recipients seem ready to take direct suggestions, voicing impatience with the hesitant, vaguely implied "need for improvement."

The declarative sentence is the stock-in-trade of every report-writer. Just as its name implies, such a unit is a statement, whether of fact or opinion; it is not a question, an exclamation, or a directive. Because it is the most frequently used sentence form, it needs all the variations of length and inner sequence of which it is capable.

Clauses and phrases may be combined in any of a number of ways. A dependent clause may come first:

When the delay in contract completion was noted, a new deadline was set.

It is the type of word that introduces the idea that controls its dependence (a subordinate conjunction like "when," "although," "while," or "after"). By reversing the same declaration, the independent thought could be put first. There may be more than one of either kind of clause in the combination. Two or more independent thoughts may be tied together by different kinds of connectives (a coordinate conjunction like "but," "and," or "however"). Such combinations come about instinctively rather than by grammatical contrivance, finding their way not only into declarative statements but also into questions and commands:

If the program is extended, what is the final cutoff date?

Extend the program but establish a cutoff date.

Phrases (groups of words without their own subjects and predicates) may also be inserted at the beginning, middle, or end of declarative sentences or of any of the classifications:

For timely completion, planning is essential.

Planning for timely completion is essential.

Planning is essential for timely completion.

As is true of the clause, there are different kinds of phrases: prepositional ("by means of controls"), adverbial ("adversely classified"), and participial ("controlling income and outflow"), for example. All sorts of phrases, just like all sorts of clauses, may be arranged in different relationships to produce diversity. "Staccato style" is not necessary in functional writing.

Change of pace

Even more useful than the grammatical classifications of sentence structure is a psychological basis for changing the pace of the coverage. Some statements are direct in impact, offering rapid-fire reading:

Analysis of the cycle's breakdown leaves us in doubt with respect to certain elements within the total 140.2 cycle.

The key element here is "Analysis of the cycle's breakdown," without which all the rest would be meaningless. The direct sequence speeds up the intake, presenting the essential item head on. Theoretically, it fits modern times, with the demand for instant replay.

Unvaried directness will, however, prove monotonous ("rat-a-tat-tat"). Furthermore, by going so fast the writer may outdistance the reader. If, at times, an indirect approach is followed, the first words will not always be the key ones:

With respect to certain elements within the total 140.2 cycle, analysis of the cycle's breakdown leaves us in doubt.

This is not the head-on attack, but a gradual, indirect one, giving readers a chance to think along with the writer, to become involved in the thought process, and to arrive at the conclusion (the key element) for themselves. This sort of indirect construction is the "think-along sentence."

Inversion is the ultimate illustration of indirectness, in which the payoff point is obviously suspended:

Although belatedly, the problems noted in the prior review have been resolved.

Once in a while, an inverted thought intrigues the reader.

Neither the direct nor the indirect type of sentence should be employed to the exclusion of the other. Most writers by nature tend either to one or the other without planned intermixing. Proper proportioning of the two kinds should set a pace that is motivating, ruling out any sense of push (from unvaried directness) or of drag (from unvaried indirectness). Neither abruptness nor hesitancy of tone is conducive to getting agreement.

In choosing how many of one kind of sentence to use versus the other, sensitivity to the subject matter and assessment of the reader's reactions constitute the controlling factors. It is the judicious intermix that counts as far as interest is concerned. Readers need a change of pace, and the sentence pattern is a means to that end.

SENSE AND SIMPLICITY

As the means to clarity, the sentence is the unit of style in greatest need of correction. Its vulnerabilities are most exposed when it is overloaded with words, ideas, or interrelationships.

"One idea to a sentence" is good advice provided there is reasonable interpretation as to what constitutes an idea. Unity is what the reader wants to derive between one capital letter and one period. When the idea is in itself complicated, the communication process must be all the more simple.

If the idea requires built-in qualification, as may be the case in operational audits, subordination of one thought to another offers more for the reading time than mere coupling.

Though the short sentence requires less effort for both writer and reader, in formal reports it should be complete in content and construction. When read aloud for testing, it should stand on its own feet, sounding neither run-on (two thoughts without a connecting word or proper punctuation) nor telegraphic (over-compressed, with the usual small words missing).

As a concomitant of the overloaded or the incomplete unit, there are a half dozen roadblocks that commonly interfere with the sense. Though the whole range of grammatical errors contains far more, the six which are found most often in functional writing as sources of confusion are the ambiguous pronoun, the dangling participle, disagreement in number, the misplaced modifier, nonparallelism, and what has been described here as the phenomenon of pyramiding.

Once the problems of length and structure have been brought under control, mere brevity and clarity can be enhanced by variety in the sentence pattern. Reading report drafts aloud will reveal monotony. Revision can then introduce as many of the available kinds of sentences as suitable. To encourage receptivity to difficult content and to be convincing about deficiencies, reports should offer a change of pace. The readers' degree of familiarity and their preparedness to agree or disagree are the criteria for pace-setting. Then the proportion of hurry-up and slow-down sentences is up to the writer's best judgment. Simple, sensible sentences are the product of careful, conscious sentence construction.

Churchill, describing his own hard schooling in the English language, which was to mean so much to him (and to the world), wrote: "... I got into my bones the essential structure of the ordinary ... sentence—which is a noble thing."[2]

NOTES

[1] Robert Frost, quoted in *Think*, vol. 31, no. 5, September–October 1965, p. 26.

[2] Winston S. Churchill, *My Early Life*, Charles Scribner's Sons, New York, 1930, p. 17.

4 Putting paragraphs together

Of all the component parts that make up a report, the paragraph has proved the easiest for everyday writers. The success with which most handle it for the consumption of readers-in-a-hurry comes from the comparatively few techniques required.

FUNCTIONAL ASPECTS

Two criteria sum up the auditor's need in turning out a readable paragraph: brevity and unity. The first criterion is for visual ease; the second is for mental ease. Though the idea of unity does carry over from school to office, the value of brevity is not stressed in all classrooms.

BREVITY

Once an author sees the "look" of short paragraphs on a page as contrasted with a solid wall of print, there is no doubt about the value of limiting the number of grouped lines. When a mass of material is divided into its constituent pieces, the reader's reluctance to dig in is reduced. "Divide and rule" is the way to hold attention, if for no other reason than sheer appeal to the eye. Psychological motivation is at stake, but it cannot and need not be achieved at the expense of logic.

First impressions

Subjectively, short-looking paragraphs tell readers they will be rewarded for their concentration with a series of significant observations or conclusions. Frequent indention or "blocking" of the first line gives a breather in the mental exertion of following difficult, arguable, or dull points. The white space provides light at the end of the tunnel. At the opening and the closing positions of a communication, such as a letter, memo, or report, readers are eased in and out by the sight of just a few grouped lines. That is where the psychological conduciveness to read plays its part. First impressions come from looking before the act of reading itself commences.

By contrast, the highly creative writers James Joyce and William Faulkner, neither of whom took as his aim easy reading, purposely wrote long, rambling paragraphs. Joyce, in his precedent-setting *Ulysses*, was pulling together all the thoughts that passed through the mind of his leading character in the course of one day. Joyce's intent was just the opposite of making such material comprehensible on the surface. In such a "stream of consciousness" there are, in actuality, no paragraphs. Though auditors have their own free flow of passing thoughts, they are not engaged in extracting unuttered or unutterable notions when writing reports. No more are report-writers engaged in making their readers discover implications that are purposely obscured or buried, which was the intent of William Faulkner and James Joyce in their lengthy paragraphs. Great as the satisfaction may be in perusing the masterpieces of literary invention on one's own time, consumers of paperwork in the office do not want to make their way through line after line of hidden mysteries, undivided and unsignaled.

By the opposite token, the everyday writer's gift to a reader consists of predigested ideas which have been sorted out and packaged ahead of time. This means presenting on a page the image of an orderly succession of points, thus feeding in the information by small mouthfuls that are easily and quickly swallowed.

Number of lines

As to how short a short paragraph should be, the measure is not in the number of sentences but in the number of lines. The sentence itself is variable in length, the line less so. The simplicity or intricacy of content is another variable. A rough average, derived over recent years from several thousands of pages of as many different auditors, comes out at seven lines per paragraph, though the upward range extends to twenty or more. Whether single or double spacing is used and whether the margin is narrow or wide, the packaged lines should convey a small block of thought, not a massive confrontation.

One rule of grammar, often remembered but also often ignored in presentations, is this: Don't write one-sentence paragraphs. The quick thinker should ask: Why not? Of course, one-sentence paragraphs should not be overdone; not every sentence deserves equal emphasis. Memos and letters should and do start and end this way often. Schoolchildren whose analytical skills need development may have to be encouraged to put together more than one sentence to prove they can. Not so their elders. The trained adult's capacity for seeing interrelationships is so well developed that the encouragement needed is in the reverse direction: to pull apart the interwoven ideas for swift comprehension. In transmitting informative or analytical details to others, it becomes essential to find the subunits within the larger unit rather than reproducing on paper a stream of consciousness.

Nonexistent in thinking and in speaking, the paragraph is a purely artificial device of the written word. If that written word is intended for functional purposes, the device performs its best service by being controlled in length.

Brevity calls attention to a point by isolating it. When too many paragraphs that are too short follow on one another's heels, a fragmented impression is possible. Readers may lose the direction of the whole message. The remedy is to give them a helping hand across the pages.

Interconnections

Shortening of paragraphs has to be accompanied by the linking technique (transition). Where one thought ends, the next must obviously follow from what has preceded. Linking between paragraphs is accomplished either explicitly or implicitly.

Explicit transition comes when the same word or group of words appears at the tail of one paragraph and at the head of the next, as here:

> The new process, if properly implemented, should provide top management with data useful in performance evaluation. The process, to be effectively applied within a work center must first be accepted by the supervisors themselves.
>
> To obtain the reactions of the supervisors to their initial use of the new evaluative method, we distributed a questionnaire....

Explicit linking, illustrated in the repetition of the word "supervisors," as well as the word "new," is instinctive with most report-writers, especially near the beginning of a report as they lead themselves and their readers at the same time over the progression of paragraphs.

Linking can also be achieved implicitly without verbatim carry-over.

The ideas then must flow so obviously from one to the next that the momentum of the logic will suffice. A writer can, without using the same word or words, keep the reader on the track. Such a method, at its best, guides by letting the interconnections reveal themselves rather than by being pointed out. What readers see for themselves they believe most readily. The risk of the implicit approach, unlike a spelled-out transition, is that some readers may lose their foothold and fall down in between the paragraphs. Use of "this" to start a sentence is, as has been recognized, often too risky.

Designators

A "surefire" way of linking is to number or letter each unit of thought, a practice followed by many military agencies and also by some civilian organizations in industry as well as in government. Each major paragraph is given an alphabetical or numerical symbol; then each subunit is given its own distinguishing designation, down to as many levels as desired. For instance:

1. paragraph
  a. paragraph
  b. paragraph
    (1) paragraph
    (2) paragraph
	A. paragraph
	  1. paragraph
	    a. paragraph
	    b. paragraph
	  2. paragraph

In this manner, a certain logic is enforced by the descending scale of importance of the paragraphs. Such a mechanical system of dividing may, by the very sense of enforcement, lessen the writer's attempt to show the inherent relationship of ideas. It may preclude the sense of self-discovery for the reader. The effect is coercive but undeniably clear.

The designation of paragraphs by letters and numbers has its pros and cons. It facilitates specific reference ("See paragraph A, 1, b") without reidentification of the substance itself. It interrelates material according to varying levels of significance. It provides a sense of outline. At the same time, it seems to result in longer units, which is not an advantage. For instance, a writer may see how one long paragraph, labeled "A," could be divided into two parts (between the major point and one minor supporting point), but that writer may be unable to find a second minor point. Thus the problem arises of having an "A" with only a "1" as the subparagraph and no "2." This creates a dilemma in logic. Whatever is subdivided is assumed to have a minimum of two subparts. The use of "A" itself sets the reader up for a "B," just as a "1" sets the reader up for at least a "2."

With or without labels, short paragraphs are an invitation to the reader to enter the communication process. The page laid out with oases of white space offers the promise of getting somewhere, each step leading to the succeeding one. Whether one line or seven, whether one sentence or more, there is visual inducement. The only technique required for brevity is to find and act upon the natural breakpoints.

UNITY

Three techniques ensure unification of the one thought to which a paragraph must be restricted: spanning, linking, and wrapping up. These three belong in the beginning, the middle, and the end, respectively. If so incorporated, these techniques will produce at the paragraph level the same sense of continuity that arises in the total report (or section thereof) from the use of a spanning introduction, an interlinked midsection, and a concluding wrap-up. Psychological and logical flow within each paragraph, long or short, rests on the same idea of cohesiveness as the total document. For the occasional one-sentence paragraph there is no problem, but the longer the unit, the more helpful the three techniques become.

Spanning

To get started on a new thought, the reader depends upon a lead sentence that is a reliable indicator of everything that is to follow before the final period:

> In researching the problem of reducing the size of the quality-assurance files, two systems were found to be in use to reduce and manipulate large amounts of data.

This "topic sentence," as it is familiarly known, tips the reader off to the pursuant identification of both systems. The opener has to be constructed like an umbrella that is of just the right proportions.

If its circumference extends beyond the coverage required for the sentences that come under it, the reader may feel overwhelmed at the outset and is sure to feel let down at the end:

> The total administrative staff was classified by function: production, service, finance, and public relations. The financial administrators were compensated according to their specified duties such as accounting and forecasting. As a result there were varying rates of pay within their classification.

Readers are left without gratification of their natural curiosity as to the other three groups named.

More often, a writer starts a paragraph with a sentence that provides too little protection for the thoughts that crowd together before a break on the page is permitted. The spanner, in that case, does not fully span. In such a situation, what has happened is probably this: The writer thinks there is one neat little unit that can be covered by an even neater little statement and, as a result, opens with something that is more like a parasol, providing too little protection for all the sentences flocking together beneath it:

> In the third quarter, earnings rose sharply. They exceeded the calculations which were projected in the regular manner. In the first quarter of the year, earnings were slightly above the estimate, though they fell in the second quarter and are being projected on a slightly different basis for the fourth quarter.

All four quarters have been covered, though the first sentence refers only to the third. Here, the auditor's material got out of hand and strayed too far from the protection of the umbrella. The thoughts of a knowledgeable writer often flow more rapidly than expected. The solution is easy: Either divide the paragraph into two or more paragraphs and reunify them, or reconstruct the opening sentence to achieve both continuity and brevity with one stroke of the pen.

Readers-in-a-hurry are apt to skim a report by glancing at the first sentence of each paragraph. If these have been rightly constructed, the reader's legitimate expectations of getting an overall notion of the whole document are fulfilled. If not, the writer has lost one chance to provide comprehension of the major points.

Paragraphs that lack a topic sentence are as difficult to follow as those which open misleadingly. Such a lack occurs without authors' realizing it because the spanning sentence remains lodged in their own minds. They forget altogether to dislodge the essence of that overall thought from their own minds and put it down on the paper in front of them. Readers then are forced to read not only between the lines but between the paragraphs. An example of such a "sin" of omission (rather than commission) is this:

> In one instance, supplies were delayed en route. In another, equipment needed for making repairs was not delivered to the loading dock. All orders had been placed with the same vendor.

The reader, having conscientiously perused each sentence, now has to backtrack, searching for the common factor between the three sentences. In the example quoted, the revision consists of inserting as the opener:

> Use of a sole-source vendor resulted in delays.

With this addition the true significance of the original two sentences is made clear, with the third turning into an effective wrap-up. An umbrella has been raised.

Checkpoints regarding the topic sentence which functional writers need to observe are these:

1. Be sure to raise an umbrella of some kind.
2. Push out the umbrella if it proves too small in circumference.
3. Draw in the umbrella if it extends beyond what is placed under it.

Linking

Just as links are needed between consecutive paragraphs, connections are needed between successive sentences to establish intraparagraph unity. Churchill expressed the need by drawing an analogy: "Just as the sentence contains one idea in all its fullness, so the paragraph should embrace a distinct episode; and as sentences should follow one another in harmonious sequence, so the paragraphs must fit on to one another like the automatic couplings of railway carriages."[1]

Too much or too obvious reliance upon explicit linking sometimes annoys because of excessive repetition of the same words or phrases. It gives readers the impression of talking down rather than building up:

> Central inventory control records are valuable. Central inventory control records provide. . . .

A less obvious but still explicit version would be:

> Central inventory control records are valuable. Such records. . . .

It is up to the writer to judge how much help is required and how much will be taken as an insult. If the subject is diversified or is devoid of apparent relationships, more explicitness is acceptable.

Linking, when combined with a well-fitted topic sentence, speeds up reading time. The combination enables the report-writer to avoid a frequent trap: the use of worn-out, mechanical "tie" words, like "also," "in addition," and "as a result," at the beginning of sentences. Overuse of any expression weakens its signaling power. At times, such connectives are even illogically inserted when a point is not really an addition to, or a result of, what has been stated. They resemble an automatic reflex action rather than a well-thought-out sequence. Characteristically, when "also" appears as the first word in the last sentence of a paragraph, it reveals a lack of forethought in the topic sentence. When the groundwork has been properly laid at that stage, there is no need to drag in an "also ran" point. On the occasions when such trite terms seem unavoidable, they can be moved away from the position of emphasis at the head of a sentence and buried in the middle. Instead of:

> Also, the records were incomplete.

it would be better, if the meaning is not altered, to say:

> The records were also incomplete.

Misuse of the first position of emphasis in a sentence often occurs with other "favorites" like "Enclosed is. . . ." and "Attached are. . . ." The reader wants to know what is enclosed and how the enclosure correlates with surrounding content. All that is needed is to put the horse before the cart:

> The copy of the requested site investigation is enclosed.

The opportunity for opening emphasis is also washed when a mere reference source, instead of the substance of the reference, stands first:

> Federal Regulations 45 CFR 205.150 require the agencies to establish and maintain methods and procedures for properly sharing costs.

This, too, can be improved merely by putting "methods and procedures" first, before the necessary but less meaningful source. If the same mechanical terms are implanted no matter what the subject, they will supply less specific relevance as connectives.

Ideally, implicit transition may be built in as the underlying unit so that repetition of the same wording and mechanical linking are diminished or eliminated:

> Regulations provide that, if the branch's chief officer is to be absent because of leave or transfer, the assistant is to assume responsibility. Recording inventories, submitting requisitions, and authorizing payments must proceed on schedule. Signature of either individual is to be regarded as acceptable in such transactions.

The techniques of spanning and linking are both demonstrated, yet no word has been restated, and the machinery of the communication process is not heard knocking. The flow of thought is smooth when transitions are self-evident. Only a few cautions are necessary:

1. Guard against loopholes in fact or reasoning that cannot be bridged by any form of linking. The only solution is to fill in the gap with the missing explanation.

2. Do not hesitate to use explicit linking between sentences when the material is closely packed.

3. Vary the explicitness, which necessarily means using the same words, by showing implicit relationships between the content of one sentence and that of the next.

4. Resort to the mechanical, all-too-familiar, trite connectives only when more specific terms prove impossible. Let real logic speak for itself.

Wrapping up

The one-sentence paragraph needs only itself as its own umbrella. The paragraph of more than one sentence that is held within a few lines needs only the linking and spanning techniques. For units of greater length and complexity, one more aid is available: a short wrap-up at the end.

Such an addition will pull back together the preceding sentences, each of which constitutes a subpoint of the opener. By pulling together the overriding idea at the end position, the writer leaves the final emphasis where it is desired. Readers then undertake the next paragraph with a feeling of relief and confidence, as would be true in this detailed discussion:

> Cash receipts were not promptly deposited in the bank. Section X on page 2 of the instruction stipulates that all cash receipts be deposited intact daily. In the period March 18, 19____, to April 14, 19____, there were 12 days on which there were collections from twenty-five individuals. For these 12 days one deposit of $3423.09 was made to the bank. From April 17, 19____, to May 29, 19____, there were 14 days of collections during which only one deposit was made ($1016.62). All cash receipts should be deposited daily.

The reader may proceed to the next problem with a firm grasp of the need for better deposit practices.

The last sentence is sometimes, though rarely, used for another purpose: as the topic sentence. Literature offers many examples of details that are unfolded and unified only at the end in a sort of upside-down umbrella. As an occasional variant on tradition, the device may be carried over from literary style to functional style. Its effect is at best one of variation, but such an overturn to a reader's conditioned expectations is questionable. Besides, a "treasure hunt" paragraph of this kind takes more time to write as well as to read. Experienced, professional writers may heighten interest by doing things differently. For those with less experience, observance of traditions is a bond with the recipients.

Typically, the last sentence should reassemble the bits and pieces justifying the first. The more bits and pieces there are, the more the short payoff statement at the end contributes.

TWO PROBLEMS

A consistent approach pattern in a report is essential if the readers are to follow from beginning to end. Effortless reading rests in part upon compatibility of references to time and to perspective.

Establishing time frames

For safety's sake, factual observations are usually reported as being restricted to a given period in the past. Auditors are not necessarily held responsible for the verifiability of the cited conditions after the cutoff date of the review. This being the case, the action words (verbs) should usually refer back by means of the past tense. Deciding upon such a policy facilitates uniformity not only when one writer is involved but more particularly when a whole team is working on the total report. The verbs in this paragraph, reporting on factual observations, are in the past tense:

> Most of the building projects we saw were of good appearance. In general, the projects were self-liquidating.

When "had" is inserted (to make the tense past perfect), the verb then refers to an action completed in the past at a time preceding another past action:

> Most of the facilities which we had seen at the time of our prior inspection had been in good repair at that time. During the subsequent visit, we observed that the facilities were not in good repair.

Matters such as judgments, recommendations, and conclusions may be stated in the present tense because they genuinely refer to a subsequent point in time:

> We believe the objectives of the building projects can be achieved if the rate of inflation remains the same.

Recommendations and other projected ideas are also sometimes properly expressed as related to the future or the conditional future:

> Cost estimates will need to be revised for the coming year.
>
> Cost estimates should be revised for the coming year.

Reference to the same period in time should be made in the same tense of the verb. Unconscious switching back and forth is apparent in operational reporting, but less so in financial material. It may lead to inaccuracy and is certainly confusing to the reader:

> Of the resolved complaints 36.2 percent involved delayed mail (lost mail accounted for the highest percentage, 37.5) and almost one-third of the delays is attributable to carrier mishandling.

Obviously, the reasons for the complaints were tabulated at the same time, so the past tense ("involved" and "accounted") should have carried through to the third and last reason where the present tense ("is") slipped in.

Examples of unintentional tense switching, when the same period is meant, are so numerous in operational audit writing that the reasons must be deep-seated. Auditors' strong sense of conditions noted during the audit work seems to persuade them of indeterminate but unproved continuation, and the present tense creeps into the reporting process. Perhaps the facts being reported are of such long standing as to seem continuously prevalent, even though there is no need to vouch for what happens after the cutoff date. Perhaps the notes jotted down in the workpapers during the course of the investigation make their way into the draft without being revised to fit the tense of surrounding verbs. Perhaps the present tense seems more emphatic. Whatever the cause for the unconscious mixture of past, present, and future in reporting on the same period, readers lose their way, and writers expose themselves to accountability they need not assume.

Justifiable change of tense is based on bona fide distinctions between different periods:

> When we examined the facilities, we noted lack of maintenance. In our opinion, such a lack is uneconomic in the long run. Our estimate of costs indicates that provision of daily upkeep will be less expensive than construction of new quarters.

In changing from the past ("examined" and "noted"), the writer gave a signal before switching into the present ("in our opinion"). Another signal ("Our estimate") was provided before the future tense.

Unintentional tense switching can be caught during self-revision if the draft is set aside to cool. A change of tense would appear necessary for the italicized words in this sentence:

> We *would appreciate having* your comments once you *had* an opportunity to evaluate the proposal *being made.*

This inconsistency too would have been self-evident.

> Progress reports covering the work on the project segments *have not been submitted* after the project's work periods *had expired.*

Once an author gets off the track, it is hard to get back.

Intentional switching can be clarified by notifying the reader of the passage of time. Over the longer unit of style, the paragraph, extra watchfulness is needed for the smooth, chronological flow.

Setting perspectives

The approach pattern from which the pilot of an airplane starts a landing must be plotted in advance and unswervingly followed lest an emergency be created. In paragraphing, the "pilot" is likewise advised to start from a planned perspective and to adhere to it so that the readers will not be thrown off course.

If the approach (that is, the perspective from which a subject is to be covered) is to be personalized, the first person plural ("we," "us," "our," and "ours") should be introduced near the beginning, maintained as reminders in the middle, and come in at the final stage. The first person singular ("I," "me," "my," and "mine"), though rare in formal reports, may be suitable as a means of keeping the reader in the line of vision in the paragraphs of a memo or letter. More typically, the plural "we" is used to denote the team aspect of auditing.

An even more personalized tone is conveyed if the second person ("your," "your," and "yours") is also included. Then the reader gets the sound of a human voice behind the print on the page. The last paragraph is the likeliest to contain a "you," very often in a transmittal, but sometimes in the end of the report itself:

> You are requested to reply within the next 30 days to the recommendations we are submitting for your approval.

If the second person is to be needed at the close or elsewhere, it should appear first in the opening paragraph or at least near the beginning so that the readers will feel they are being addressed by the same personalized voice from start to finish.

Though not always recognized, "you" is involved throughout those reports which state the recommendations in the imperative form of the verb like a command:

> Install the new equipment.
>
> Arrange for observation for a trial period.
>
> Check the quality of finished goods.

"You" is understood as the subject of the imperative verbs "Install," "Arrange," and "Check."

The impersonal perspective excludes all but the third person: "he," "him," "his," "she," "her," "hers," "it," "its," "they," "them," "their," and "theirs." The impersonal approach, which is the sign of formality in reporting, avoids naming names and instead identifies names of positions like "partner," "director," or "chief." If this is the approach to be taken, there should be no lapses into inconsistent pronouns of the first and second persons. It may even be necessary for writers to speak of themselves not as "we" but as "the audit staff" or "the auditors." Even such legalistic use of the third person can still stay away from the stiffness of "the undersigned" or "the writer."

Person switching is just as distracting as tense switching. Readers look for a clue at the beginning to help them determine the approach pattern that is to be followed throughout. Once it is established, they do not expect the point of view to jump around, as happened in this preaudit survey:

> Until now, I have not been aware of what ledgers to examine. You can consider several alternatives. The choice one makes depends upon the availability of all ledgers.

Who, exactly, is going to do the examining, the considering, and the choosing? The first person ("I"), the second person ("you"), or the third person ("one")?

Consistency of either the personal or the impersonal approach is created by control of the first, second, and third person pronouns (both *within* and *between* paragraphs) from the beginning to the end of a whole communication.

EASE OF IMPLEMENTATION

The problems of the paragraph are minimal compared with those of the sentence. If the time frame is accurately established and the perspective is clearly set, unity is easier. All that remains besides achieving brevity and unity is to abide by the customary technique of a strong lead sentence with maintenance of links between the sentences that fit together under that "umbrella."

NOTES

[1] Winston S. Churchill, *My Early Life*, Charles Scribner's Sons, New York, 1930, pp. 211–212.

5 Punctuating for guidance

Punctuation is another of the technical means assisting reader and writer alike. It is, of course, inseparable from style as a whole, including all component parts of a report. Its careful incorporation in the sentence and in the paragraph pays off in the opportunity afforded to the reader to pause and reflect. For rapid coverage, punctuation marks should serve as traffic signals.

TRAFFIC SIGNALS

As automatic checkpoints, established marks perform the same function as "Stop," "Go Slow," and "Right Turn Only" signs. Without such directions, or with misdirections, thoughts collide. Certain signs that are of particular guidance can still be particularly misleading.

Apostrophe

For some reason the humble little apostrophe is suffering from neglect. It is simply ignored by those who write in haste or uncertainty. Yet this one elevated comma may make a critical difference, as one auditor-author came to realize where a large sum was at stake:

> It is essential to calculate quarterly expenditures. After April, only the current months addition will be considered.

An apostrophe either before or after the "s" in "months" would have made it possible to tell whether the calculation would take into consideration 1 current month or 3 current months (that is, a quarter). If the mark is placed before the "s" ("the current month's addition"), the singular possessive is shown (1 month); if it is placed after the "s" ("the current months' addition"), the plural possessive is shown (several months). No such ambiguity arose in this correct example:

> The report includes present year's actual costs and future year's budgeted costs.

It is clear that only 2 years are included together.

In pluralizing certain numbers or abbreviations, the apostrophe is also a guide:

> The count was made in batches by 500's.
>
> Troops were classified by their military specialties into MOS's.

In abbreviations not ending in an "s," clarity does not seem to suffer when the apostrophe is dropped:

> The organization of CPAs is named the American Institute of Certified Public Accountants.

For contractions, the same mark is used in the place of the omitted letters, as in "don't," "we've," "haven't," and "isn't." The abbreviated form for years may be handled like contractions: "1980" becomes "'80." An exception to the rule on contractions involves the troublesome words "its" and "it's," which are a possessive and a contraction, respectively; both would take the apostrophe if the rule were to apply. To distinguish the two uses, the mark is retained only for the contraction and is not employed for the possessive. The contraction reads:

> In view of the deadline for the report, it's overdue.

The possessive of the same pronoun reads:

> The report contains six findings between its covers.

Colon

The colon is one of the most valuable marks in practical material because of the strict control it exercises. It gives a clear direction. The sight of it means that a long quotation, a long listing, or a long explanation is coming. Next to the period, it provides the most definite break:

The report contains three recommendations:

1. _____
2. _____
3. _____

Nine times out of ten the colon implies the same thing as mechanical linking words like "the following," "as follows," and "cited below." These words usually can be cut as redundant because the colon says it all.

Occasionally, the colon separates two main clauses if the second clause provides explanation or amplification of the first:

> The mirror needed wherein auditors can see themselves is three-way: They will see themselves as professional auditors, as team members representing their employing organizations, and as individual human beings.

As a minor matter, the colon is also the tradition after the salutation in American business letters (though the comma is used in some countries).

Comma

The workhorse of punctuation is the comma. Its principles are multiple, though their practice is often questionable.

One of the most frequent mistakes is the absence of one of a logical pair of commas around an explanatory insertion:

> The unexpected supplies, received late were not accompanied by an invoice.

After "late" another comma is needed as the back fence; the front fence (after "supplies") is in place. Just as often, the front fence is lacking, though the back fence is in place. This example has both halves of the proper pair:

> The survey will, as a start, cover more ground than the final audit.

Another logical principle to be used when enclosing content is essential in that it conveys possible legal implications. When points have to be qualified or restricted, the restricting words are not separated by commas from what they restrict, as this sentence correctly shows:

> Staff members who had seniority were granted pay increases.

The clause "who had seniority" exercises strict limitation over the number of staff members receiving the raises. The author would not have been willing to imply that all staff members were granted pay increases.

To complete this reasoning, other additions which could be dropped without producing inaccuracy (nonrestrictive elements) must be surrounded by commas:

> The five members of the Senior Staff, who had enjoyed their association with the firm, were ex officio members of the executive committee.

Their "enjoyment" may be of interest, but if the "who" clause were not present, the five would still be ex officio members. Another statement illustrates an addition which could not be dropped without producing inaccuracy (restrictive element):

> The files which were reviewed in the investigation showed no discrepancies.

In connection with the distinction between restrictive and nonrestrictive elements, an old-fashioned, seldom-observed, but worrisome distinction between "that" and "which" sometimes comes to mind. The first of the two words formerly was reserved for restrictive clauses, and the second for nonrestrictive clauses:

> The accounts that were reviewed were up to date.

The clause "that were reviewed" is restrictive. By contrast, a nonrestrictive clause begins with "which":

> The accounts, which were numerous, were up to date.

Such discrimination might be useful if regularly practiced; it is not. One English authority, in discussing the two words, commented wryly: "What grammarians say should be has perhaps less influence on what shall be than even the more modest of them realize...."[1]

One moot point concerning the comma relates to the final item in a series. Although a series of words, phrases, or clauses must be divided by commas, the mark is optional before the "and" or "or" introducing the last item. For speedy, self-confident writing it would be wise to set a policy, either for or against. If the decision is against, there must be room for exceptions. In a long and complicated series, the reader will appreciate the mark before "and," as illustrated:

> Manufacturing was held up by absence of personnel due to strikes, subsequent reduction in the first-quarter profits, and overall inability to supply the market before competitors.

Another instance requiring the comma before the "and" arises when one of the items in the array itself contains an inner "and." Here, the author made it impossible to determine what was included in each of four elements apparently being designated:

> Four elements are essential to support maintenance: these are reparable assets, repair parts, funds, and facilities, and equipment.

The first two items in the series are obvious: (1) "reparable assets" and (2) "repair parts." But the third item might be "funds" or "funds and facilities." If the latter alternative is the real meaning, the original comma would have to be cut between those words. The fourth item is equally unclear. It might be "equipment" or "facilities and equipment." If the latter alternative is the real meaning, the original comma would have to be cut between those words.

Commas are sometimes mistakenly thrown in after the equating conjunction "and" or "but" at the beginning of a clause (or sentence), but there is no rule or reason for doing so.

One less confusing rule is that a comma should be used to separate independent clauses in a sentence before the joining word (such as "and," "but," "or," "nor," or "for"). It is not invariably needed, as when the independent clauses are short and simple:

> The auditors were on time and the company's representatives were also prompt.

In another sentence, however, ambiguity arises unless a comma is added to show the start of the second independent clause:

> An empty drum had to be removed from the rack and the lid and the shaft had to be changed to the full drum.

A comma before the first "and" is essential to indicate where the one step ended and the other began.

Economy of punctuation is the trend in spite of the rule calling for a comma after an introductory word, phrase, or clause. Even when the opener consists of one word or a short phrase, many readers automatically expect a breakpoint, as included in:

> Furthermore, deadlines were met.

> As a result, regulations were applied.

When such openers are complicated or long, the breakpoint is a relief. Yet writers sometimes waive the rule without harm:

> In recording the inventory we double-checked the drug stocks.

No need is felt for a comma after "inventory" even though the word ended the introductory phrase.

Among the miscellaneous services performed by the comma is the setting off of names, titles, dates, and figures:

> The two top officers, the Chairman of the Board and the President, were both recorded as in attendance at the meeting.
>
> The period reviewed, September 1 through September 30, 19_____, was not comparable to the same period in the previous fiscal year.
>
> The total amount expended, $30,129, was broken down by months.

Such pairs of commas surround wording in apposition with preceding wording (to put it another way, wording that means the same as something else named).

The comma serves before short quotations of a whole sentence or sentences (though the colon is the stronger indicator before a long selection). If the quotation is less than a whole sentence and is woven in by a word such as "that," even the comma is superfluous:

> The regulation prescribed that "logs which are kept daily" should be signed. The regulation goes further by adding, "Summaries of such logs should also be signed."

A comma is erroneous when it intrudes, as it is apt to do, between subject and predicate (the main verb), either immediately or with intervening words:

> The storage of controlled substances, needed tighter security.

The simple subject, "storage," should not be split from its predicate (the verb), "needed," regardless of intervening modification ("of controlled substances"). In an initially correct sentence, addition of a comma after the subject ("investigation") would be illogical:

> A site investigation requires special planning.

Dash

The dash performs a less well defined function, being often thrown into the breach for lack of certainty about how else to punctuate. As one commentator wrote after an excerpt from the published letters of an actor:

> Hurry Scurry as usual
> What a scrawl—always in a hurry.

"Postscripts of this kind abound in the letters of David Garrick. His punctuation, consisting largely of dashes, gives an air of breathless haste...."[2]

Strictly employed, the dash (whether one, two, or three straight lines) indicates a break in sentence structure, an attention-getting device not common in everyday prose:

What we need is authority—authority to carry out the investigation.

While seeming to stop after the first "authority," the writer decided to start up again for renewal of emphasis. Breaking structure, like any device, quickly loses its effect if overused.

A dash, loosely tossed in, blurs precision. Writers who depend upon it instead of figuring out the more exact mark sacrifice clarity. Its very versatility has reduced its specific quality within a paragraph or sentence. The reader gets easier direction from tighter punctuation. If the desire is for open-ended, do-it-yourself interpretation, the dash will accomplish that game plan. Used in default of something better, the dash is not defensible.

Hyphen

The hyphen tells another story. Its utility is increasing with the endless diversification of subject matter. It ties two or more words together so that, at first glance, no time is lost in seeing the connections. Compound modifiers are a necessity in many descriptive terms:

draft-motivated enlistment

follow-up review

single-location survey

mass-produced corridor panels

cost-plus-fixed-fee contract

Lacking the hyphens, the compound modifiers might each be read momentarily as separate from the others, and this would be misleading.

In many situations that have to be completely identified, the supply of single adjectives (words describing nouns or pronouns) and adverbs (words describing verbs, adjectives, or other adverbs) has been exhausted. Parts of speech have shifted back and forth from nouns and verbs to descriptive terms, no matter what the dictionaries say. Each new refinement, each further specification of content, calls for another modifier, and compounds are themselves being compounded:

the contractor-owned, government-operated facility

Without the bonding effect of the hyphen, supplemented at times with the comma or other mark, coined combinations may not be read as intended.

The hyphen is a particularly effective compromise when nouns and adjectives are joined in a pyramid of modifiers for which the unfamiliar reader has no preparation as to what word is to be related to what other word:

> Corridor connectors, first produced by XYZ Company, were part of the five-section inflatable shelters.

"Five," if it had not been joined to "section" by the hyphen, would have been applied to "shelters," making it possible that corridor connectors were part of the five shelters that were section-inflatable.

The language being historically in a state of flux, the hyphen in a compound may be a preliminary to what will become one word: A "full-time" employee may become a "fulltime" employee. Many still find it hard to read an unhyphenated word like "coinsurance." If hyphens lead the way, readers will keep up with the rapid transformation of terms required to explain minute detail.

Parentheses and brackets

Growing in popularity are parentheses. Wording so set off should be truly parenthetical (that is, expendable). As content intensifies in depth and extent, readers appreciate differentiation between what is more important and what is less so. They can, if in a hurry, skip what seems less pertinent.

The very option to read or not to read a parenthetical insert may incline readers to look at it. People read more willingly what they do not have to read. Hence may arise the notion of parentheses as a way of emphasis. As part of the benefit, the essential matter is set off from the unessential.

Parentheses enable writers to address various levels of readership as to the differing degrees of explanatory support needed:

> A direct delivery (consisting of a shipment from a vendor to the requisitioners) can be initiated by automatic processing.

Some would be in need of the definition; some would not. For definitions, examples, or details, parentheses are a way of whispering in a reader's ear, thus lowering the decibel level in crowded coverage. The density of audit material requires strategies in the communication of it.

When the parenthesized material comes at the end of a sentence of which it is an integral part, the period stands outside; when such material is a complete sentence in itself, the first parenthesis is preceded by a period, and the next period is placed inside the second parenthesis. Double punctuation, with periods both inside and out, is extravagant.

Making cross references parenthetical is also a way of reducing the inevitable distraction such references cause, no matter how necessary:

> The estimate should be increased by 16 percent. (See Exhibit A for detailed dollar adjustments.)

Not all readers will have to turn to the details. Those who do, being reassured in a subdued tone that such information is accessible, do not feel compelled to turn to it at once, thereby losing the main thread.

Less in demand are brackets. These squared enclosing marks now customarily signify supplementary material which itself contains inner parentheses:

> [Change in the end of the fiscal year (from June 30 to September 30) took into consideration budget projections.]

Brackets are also used in quoting when it is necessary for the quoter to insert clarifying wording:

> The Regulation states: "They [the responsible parties] must sign the duplicate copies."

Period

The "full stop," as the British call the period, is the most instructive of all traffic signals for readers who wish to be sure of the direction in which they are traveling. The more periods, the shorter the sentences. So long as monotony is avoided, using an abundance of periods is the quickest way to be clear. They give notice of one thought at a time. (Question marks and exclamation marks, also serving as full stops, are infrequent in audit reports.)

Seldom is the period overused. Of course, if it follows an incomplete statement, readers are quick to recognize the shortfall:

> The fiscal year being incompletely covered.

On the contrary, its omission between two independent thoughts, unrelated by a connecting word (conjunction) or spliced only by a comma, is quickly detected in sentences that are then called "run-on":

> The overstatements are caused apparently by a deliberate attempt, available appropriations had to be expended.

The period should stand where the comma is. Such a glaring grammatical fault is rare, as is the incomplete sentence. Reading drafts aloud is the best way to catch incomplete or run-on sentences.

The popular religious leader Norman Vincent Peale, who worked as a reporter in his youth, recalled a lesson he had been taught. The editor put down a dot and asked his reporter what it was. Peale answered that it was a dot. The editor replied, "No, it's a period—the greatest literary device ever created."[3]

Dots are required for another purpose when quoting only parts of a whole passage: A series of three dots shows that words have been left out from the beginning or the middle of a sentence; a series of four dots shows that words have been omitted at the end:

> An encumbrance list containing certain commitments was filed, according to the official, but "...was filed late and did not include all...commitments made for the ensuing year...."

In enumerating (the shopping-list device), periods at the end of each item are optional. When the points are expressed as complete sentences, a full stop after each may be a convenience. When they are short, open punctuation (that is, none) better conveys the overall unity while still signifying an itemization of points. The period remains customary after the final item in the listing. An even more complex and old-fashioned system involving the semicolon within a listing is hardly worth the time it takes:

> We have cash flow plans with:
>
> Emergency Control Board;
>
> Contingency Operations Staff; and
>
> Daily Issuance Office.

The semicolons and the "and" detract from the very purpose of setting off the three entities. Here is one place to economize by doing away with what will not be missed.

Periods after abbreviations, though once mandatory, are now often omitted. As one type of shortcut, most acronyms stand alone: CPA, SOP, OMB, AEP, NCR. In breaking away from any tradition, the fundamental question is whether the new form will look right to the receiver. If it will, thrift dictates the answer, not overpunctuation.

Quotation marks

In quoting directly the exact words of another person or another document, enclosing the words in double quotation marks is not only the rule but a protective measure. Yet these marks are frequently missing. It is only fair that original sources should get the credit or the blame for their own words. Failure to give the signal by these marks is, at the worst, plagiarism; at best, it is foolhardy.

If, for instance, there is a lack of clarity in regulatory language that has been lifted from a governmental or industrial publication without being so identified, the reader attributes the obscurity not to the source but to the report-writer.

As to where the quotation marks come in relation to the end punctuation of a sentence, only the stickler will insist. Printers' rules in the United States stipulate that the period (or the comma) must always come inside the quotation marks, even when only the immediately preceding words are quoted:

> The circular describes the scope of the audit as "cradle to the grave."

The rule cannot be rationalized because the period ends the whole statement, not just its closing portion. If that mark were not a period (or a comma, as within a sentence) but a colon, question mark, semicolon, or exclamation point, the mark would stand outside the quotation marks, the rational position. In British usage, all marks, including the period and the comma, stand outside. Such a curious distinction is not worth the effort to understand it. Some say the American way looks better. Either way, if followed consistently, should be satisfactory.

Verbatim quotations must be identified as such where the auditor is reproducing the auditee's comments without paraphrasing them. Restating in the slightest degree renders the marks improper. In quoting verbatim, not even an obvious slip or ambiguity can be changed, in which case quoters may disavow the blame by giving the Latin word for "thus" in parentheses or brackets:

> The Director commented to those who were not present (*sic*) that they were in violation.

"*Sic*" (underlined or italicized because it is a foreign word) implies that the passage is intentionally left as written, sensible or not. Even a spelling error is at times noted in this fashion.

Auditees' responses as incorporated in auditors' reports may extend over more than one paragraph. Setting them off by using extra indention right and left, sometimes with differentiated spacing, or by putting them in italics saves the writer from having to follow a complicated and little-known rule. It is this: In quoting consecutive paragraphs, the first paragraph and every paragraph after that must be preceded by quotation marks, but only the last paragraph, at the finish of the passage, is closed by them. Much more convenient for multiparagraph quotations is the practice of setting them off typographically or by indention.

Quotations within quotations take single quotation marks. Though a rarity in audit material, such situations occur in investigative reports:

> The safety inspector stated that he advised the employees: "Comply with the notice, 'No Smoking,' posted on the door."

If unusual wording is to be introduced, possibly very informal or very technical, the so-called apologetic quotation marks are a way of implying this. To the unfamiliar or unsuspecting reader, a special meaning is suggested:

> Standards were developed on the basis of "experience" factors common in commercial firms.

Or:

> A "skilled nursing home" is a facility which has been certified as meeting federal and state qualifications.

Or:

> The certification journals were not footed and compared with the "zebra" sheets.

The marks around such expressions are alert signals; their overuse, however, often weakens the effect.

Use of quotation marks for certain titles has been the rule, although not regularly followed. Whereas underlines have supposedly indicated major titles (books and periodicals), quotation marks have been used for minor titles (chapters in books and articles in periodicals). In recent years, the number of printed sources to be cited has grown so conspicuously that the time to carry out the underlining (double typing) may account for its general abandonment. Capital letters serve the same purpose, or even initial capitals for either major or minor titles.

Wherever underlines appear, they do add emphasis. Foreign words, except for ones that have become part of everyday English, are underlined (or italicized). Quite apart from titles, some writers have a habit of underlining or italicizing words here, there, and everywhere in the hope of getting more attention. If employed sparingly, the scheme will make a word or words jump out of the page. If this habit of shouting continues, readers turn off and cease to react.

Semicolon

Because the semicolon makes it grammatically possible to lengthen statements, it is something to employ sparingly. In two situations, it is indispensable:

1. Between equal independent elements (like clauses) where a connecting word (a coordinate conjunction) like "and" is not present:

   The personnel who were on the regular payroll were paid; the others who were part-time were not.

2. Between dependent but equal elements when there are commas within one or more of those elements:

   Of all 100 items tested, we found 82 which were operating, in part satisfactorily, in part unsatisfactorily; 12 which had not been tried; and 6 which were operating, but not within the cycled time.

In the first situation, the semicolon substitutes for the conjunction. In the second situation, it is to show the higher level of break than the lower level where the comma comes.

Misuse of the semicolon between unequal elements frequently happens when a series is being introduced (the proper mark would be the colon):

   We have identified five areas which can be classified as specialized services; contract closing statements, contract proposal evaluations, accounting system surveys, quick assessments, and system reviews.

An independent clause precedes the semicolon, whereas phrases follow it. A colon, not a semicolon, is needed after "services."

The rule of thumb by which to test the semicolon's correctness is to answer affirmatively the question: Is it separating equal elements? It must not divide an independent from a dependent clause, which was the mistake in this:

   To keep the Company's tax skirts clean, the Company cannot be billed for an asset in which it claims ownership; unless the asset was in existence at the time.

The same rule of thumb applies for correction of the prevalent mispunctuation of "however" in the middle of a sentence. If what stands before "however" and what follows are independent clauses, capable of standing alone, the semicolon is mandatory:

   The preliminary survey suggests a limited scope of audit; however, flexibility is a requisite in case of unanticipated problems.

To prove the correctness of such usage, the test is to see whether a period could take the semicolon's place; if the period could, a mere comma would be incorrect. By the same token, if a period cannot be substituted, the comma and not the semicolon becomes mandatory:

> The known problems, however, should enter into the audit program.

The differentiation is important.

Several other words like "therefore," "nevertheless," "moreover," "thus," "otherwise," and "hence" behave the same way in the middle of a sentence, and the same reasons for distinction between the semicolon and the comma apply as in the case of "however." Proper use of the semicolon appears in the first of these two statements; by contrast, the second shows the proper use of the comma:

> Procedures provided for sales accountability; nevertheless, analyses were not prepared for all merchandise.

> The subsidiary vouchers, nevertheless, supported only $5,140 of the stated amount.

Slash

Suddenly the slash (a diagonal line between two words) has begun to spread across the pages of formal as well as informal communications. Its advantage is also its disadvantage. The advantage is speed for the writer, who does not have to stop and think through the relationship between the slashed words, as in "stockholder/broker." The disadvantage is delay for the reader, who has to try to translate this many-faceted mark.

Rule books are of little help, infrequently even mentioning this latecomer to the punctuation spectrum. Without preordained regulations governing slashes, writers have rushed to its all-too-facile use. Unfortunately, what saves them the time to pin down their specific meaning costs the readers double. The mounting use of this "cop-out" is a symptom of pressure and haste. It defeats clarity as far as report-writers' intent is concerned and brevity as far as readers' time is concerned.

Even context did not answer the questions arising from such random illustrations of the slash as these:

instructor/student ratio	(to?)
accept/reject criteria	(or?)
service/maintenance	(and?)
2 days/man	(per?)

intermediate owner/prospect	(as?)
large displacement/heavy vehicles	(a definition?)
option/feature	(and/or?)
caseworker/client relationship	(with?)
hotel furniture/beds and mirrors	(for example?)

In dealing with proper names where slashes have already been incorporated, auditors cannot change them. In refraining from making up new expressions by means of slashes, practitioners of communication will force exactitude in their own thought processes and ward off others' doubts.

Punctuation marks, like other typographical indications, such as capital letters, serve as guideposts between the sender and the receiver. They show the progression of thought and blaze a trail. Their effectiveness lies less in the logic of syntax than in the psychology of conditioning. Capital letters, for instance, mean a new sentence, a proper name (and its modifier), or an abbreviation:

> At the Ford Motor Company, often represented by Fomoco, the employees of the Company number thousands.

Or:

> In England, English is spoken; in America, the language is different. Americans speak American, not the Queen's English.

SYSTEMATIZED SIGNS

Communication being based on mutuality of interpretation, readers and writers rely upon common symbols. The paragraph is the symbol of a unified thought, however briefly it is developed. Its sequence as to points in time and perspective demands a steady hand on the pen.

Like paragraphing, punctuation emerges in the course of writing, not in speaking. Well-recognized pointers must be employed on a system of understanding because they are not all explicable by logic. Familiar rules, not guesswork, are needed; without rules there is little rhyme or reason to apostrophes, colons, commas, dashes, hyphens, parentheses (and brackets), full stops (periods, question marks, and exclamation marks), quotation marks, semicolons, or even slashes.

Writers who are thoroughly conversant with systematized usage are the only ones who can afford to take liberties for the sake of economy or experimentation. The underlying question of adhering to, or deviating from, the rules is this: What will be of most help to most readers? Safety lies in systematization.

NOTES

[1] Henry W. Fowler, *A Dictionary of Modern English Usage*, 2d ed., Ernest Gowers (ed.), © Oxford University Press, 1965, p. 625. By permission of the Oxford University Press.

[2] *The Times Literary Supplement*, unsigned review of David M. Little and George M. Kahrl (eds.), *The Letters of David Garrick*, Mar. 26, 1964.

[3] *The Wall Street Journal*, May 7, 1969.

6 Considering auditors as authors

The capacity to be convincing requires that report-writers demonstrate professionalism, perceptiveness, and confidence, both in their observations and in the conclusions they set forth. The usual training as accountants is, normally, the starting point. Systematic logic, grammar, and accepted format play their part, but are not in themselves enough. All report-writers find themselves spending more time with pencil and paper in hand, some estimating as much as 80 percent of on-the-job hours. Even workpapers have become matters of public record and so require careful wording. Yet auditors seldom concentrate on training in writing to the same extent as professional writers: "Undoubtedly more capable audit work and constructive recommendations are wasted because of poor reporting than through any other single factor."[1]

The formal report, when finished, appears between covers with all the endorsement of the issuing source and the other formalized apparatus of publication from title page to possible attachments. No longer can a performance auditor prepare only the precast, short-form certificate, or even the long form or the management letter. The prescribed statement indicating compliance with regulations or fiscal accountability is not always enough in advising management. Yet there is no formula to deal with topics varying from computerization of parts inventories to the needs for family housing, from stream pollution to hospitalization of the elderly (to name a few instances).

Just as the word "auditing" has extended beyond money matters to the overview of management, including aspects of consulting and investigating, the role of the communicator has also expanded. In understanding their enlarged field, practical writers have to be self-aware. The best way to become so is to look in the mirror—the mirror of the written page. There, the self-image appears for all the world to see, though not all realize its significance.

The mirror needed wherein auditors can see themselves is three-way: They will see themselves as professional auditors, as team members representing their employing organizations, and as individual human beings. In the ability to appreciate the features reflecting these different roles, while making them compatible with one another, lies professional satisfaction.

PROFESSIONAL CHARACTERISTICS

First, what are the characteristics that show up on paper because of the *auditor's* professional image? Accounting remains at the core of most auditors' training but is no longer the whole story: "Accountants tend to be rather dull people . . . [those] who conduct audits and investigations for the GAO . . . who now include economists, engineers, management consultants and other specialists as well as accountants and lawyers, are often engaged in work and produce results that are far from dull."[2] For its specialists the General Accounting Office (GAO) has drawn on the experience of private industry and nonprofit organizations. Whatever the specific qualifications, the auditor is exact, critical but constructive, and insistent upon safeguarding what is put down on paper.

In the major departments of the federal government, audit responsibility has been placed under each department's Office of Inspector General, along with the responsibility for investigation and analysis. One of the visible results of such a consolidation, as far as language is concerned, is the spreading use of the word "audit" (and also of "finding") in the writing of investigators and analysts.

Though most "bread-and-butter" writers are subject-matter-oriented, the auditor (in the broad sense of that word) is even more so, putting the message itself ahead of the medium. Sweeping generalizations and unsupported conclusions are taboo. Loose wording is shunned. Subjective implications are frowned upon. The vocabulary may, for such reasons, become stilted and repetitive: "generally," "it seems to us," "apparently." Essential as qualifiers are, sometimes assurance is made not only doubly sure, but triply and more, as in this piece of redundancy:

> Objectives were not *always* being met primarily because of a lack of *proper* control over *some* maintenance functions.

Safeguarding is essential, but not to the point of taking away with the left hand that which is given with the right. What we see reflected in the mirror indirectly, as one seasoned "pro" commented, is "the auditor's psychological limitations and pressures." Some authorities have consequently put a ban on what they call "hedging." Others forbid such expressions as "We feel. . . . "

The carefully drafted short-form audit statement has proved its worth over the years, as some of its familiar words demonstrate: "Our examination was made in accordance with generally accepted auditing standards and, accordingly, included such tests of the accounting records and such other auditing procedures as we considered necessary in the circumstances."[3] Independent auditors writing about financial statements are not free agents, being bound by formal standards. Internal auditors, government auditors, and consultants are not bound in precisely the same way but do have their own codified standards. These standards, spelled out in the GAO's *Standards for Audit of Governmental Organizations, Programs, Activities and Functions*,[4] are customarily cited in official reports.

Apart from exactness, the tradition of reporting by exception has made the auditor a critic. This feature is prominent in the self-image. Exceptions to prescribed conditions are the essential subject, of necessity. The word "condition" itself, like the word "finding," has become negative in connotation. The use of "not," sometimes intensified into "never," is frequent. The obligation of being analytical frequently leads to an adversary posture. As a consequence, reports may sound hostile and accusatory. However, there is the possibility of reporting positive circumstances where no problems have been uncovered, a possibility that is receiving attention. Even if an operation appears effective, this acknowledgment is not seen by all as within their professional obligation. Some continue to avoid the risk of seeming to endorse the whole by expressing approval of a part.

The auditor who now accepts as part of the professional scope the inclusion of the "good" along with the "bad" automatically becomes more constructive. Issuance of an entirely favorable opinion, without any recommendation for change, remains rare. The constructiveness more commonly discernible comes from two things: balanced reporting and translation of the negative reality into the positive potentiality.

Balancing the content calls for statements of satisfactory conditions along with statements of unsatisfactory ones:

> We recognize that the $40,474 identified as unallowable expenditure transfers was not substantial in relation to the grants' totals of approximately $10.8 million. However, since we did find unallowable or undocumented transfers on twenty-eight of the sixty programs reviewed, improvements in procedures are recommended.

If the writer shows the recipient where the recipient has succeeded, failures that are pointed out get a psychological offset:

> Except for the storeroom, the inventories were properly taken "wall to wall." At the storeroom, inventory was counted in the order of the filing sequence of a stock record card file.

When it comes to the unsatisfactory or contrary matters which must be set forth, the negative can be translated to a positive alternative:

> The wall-to-wall method should be used throughout.

The psychological advantage of balancing (as distinguished from exception reporting) cannot be achieved by stereotyped statements like this:

> The total payments were generally found to be reasonable and proper. However, need exists for timely payment of discountable invoices.

The turnaround word "however" has the effect of an involuntary reflex action. Much more contributive is the tailor-made comment that identifies the favorable particulars:

> There were no cash shortages. Funds were fully accounted for, and all appeared adequate for current levels of activity.

> In the security area, two weak points were noted whereby routine controls were ignored. One cashier had made unauthorized payments for money orders, and another had given salary advances without approval.

Most often, the good news (when present) is stated before the bad. Reversing this order offers a variant:

> We reviewed assignments of 22,000 employes at 23 plants. Approximately 3,300 were misclassified in their job descriptions. Above the plant level, our review did not disclose significant problems with assignments.

Balancing is not the same thing as watering down a report, which is sometimes a symptom of organizational politics. Of course, balancing has no relevance in a case of fraud. The only precaution an investigator must take in reporting fraud or abuse is to disclose all the facts, not just those showing one side of the case.

ORGANIZATIONAL CHARACTERISTICS

In being exact, critical, and constructive, auditors' written work reveals their chosen, professional features. Other characteristics come from their employing organizations. To some extent, auditors have to hold themselves separate from the overall organizations they serve, whether these are governmental departments or private firms or companies. The fact that the head of the GAO is appointed for a 15-year, nonrenewable term insulates that key figure from possible political pressures. "Impairments" of independence must be recognized. Speaking for the private sector, the American Institute of Certified Public Accountants (AICPA) put it this way: "The independent auditor must be without bias with respect to the client under audit, since otherwise he would lack that impartiality necessary for the dependability of his findings."[5] The chief of a military audit agency described the role in this way: "The independent auditor stands in a unique position with right-of-access to all levels ... and with reporting responsibility to the very top of management."[6] Independence from management, whether internal or external, may be the most prized possession. For instance, in a federal agency dealing with health needs of the public, auditors owe no allegiance to a particular contracting hospital, though they must share a belief in the overall medical and administrative approach. The management consultant in a Certified Public Accountant (CPA) firm, engaged to systematize a company's manual record keeping, must be convinced of data processing's applicability before recommending it. The same is true of the internal auditor. There are hard-sell and soft-sell organizations; there are profit-centered and service-centered organizations. In reporting, the recipient's best interests must be defined and objectively viewed.

The reporting mission extends beyond observing and recording facts. Such may be the limit of the investigator's role, but for the auditor and consultant more is usually necessary. A judgment based on what is observed and recorded must follow. Judgment is part of the job, judgment that is supported by the facts. Certification rests on judgment. Yet even this does not constitute the end result of most operational audits. Not until a recommendation is set forth has such a report covered all its ground.

Making a recommendation is different from issuing an order. The former aim is purely advisory, not in itself managerial. It is up to the recipient of the document to concur and carry out the recommendation or not to do so. So long as the writers remain within the strict limits of an advisory capacity, they do not step into management's shoes or assume responsibilities outside their authority. Here is where independence is preserved.

INDIVIDUAL CHARACTERISTICS

The individual as such is clearly reflected in a personal style of writing. People are born and bred in different regions of the country (and of the world). All are the heirs of particular families, cultures, languages, and values. All are the products of particular training or educational institutions. In some areas of the United States, people say, 'The director would like for us to meet together." In other areas, people say, "The director would like us to meet together." Colloquialisms, of course, are related to the spoken word. Just as there is a Southern drawl and a New England "r," there is a written "accent" which shows up in word preferences, in gradations of formality or informality, in the very tone a report conveys.

When success is achieved, the individual feels the pride of authorship. As an instinctive part of everyone's need for self-expression, writing does not lend itself easily to conformity: "Even though our format is restrictive, personal writing policy still influences our written results and to a great extent our careers," commented one auditor. In fact, it is the element of originality that may make the difference between an average report and a good report, between a dull report and an interesting one. No author wants to don the mantle of official, bureaucratic, organizational style. Correctness, being a means to clarity, often is achieved in different ways. This ingredient of individuality was recognized in the official guidance issued to a military audit team: "There is no way that 'good' report language can be directed or legislated. This is probably because of the subjective nature of language, and the fact that good language means different things to different people."[7]

WRITTEN PRODUCT

What needs looking at is the whole person, whoever the writer may be. That individual is deliberately or subconsciously putting personal preferences into the writing. An auditor at the worst, as the report can show, is exact to the point of belaboring detail and vague to the point of weaseling; critical to the point of carping; or positive to the point of sugarcoating. At best, as most finished reports do reflect, the originator's image is precise, candid, and helpful in a composite, professional talent.

If the multiple role is fulfilled, the auditor's ultimate purpose is more likely to be achieved: that of producing constructive change. Once suggestions for change are activated as management's means to greater economy, productivity, or efficiency, the overall purpose is consummated. If the need for the desired changes can be met by management in some other way than is specified in the exact recommendations, then, too, the auditor's aim may be accomplished. If there is no concurrence as to ends or means, the auditor cannot rest content. Not until effective steps have been taken by management to counteract criticisms can the report-writer feel satisfied. There will be repeat audits, assist audits, and recourse to higher authority. Auditors are auditing other auditors. The document that may truly be said to be professional and to achieve its ultimate goal will result in improved managerial operations.

"Who" is the performance auditor, as the term is used? "Who" is the management consultant? "Who" is the investigator? The answer is: a specialist who often knows accounting or finance or investigative techniques, a trained analyst of various government and business activities, and an individualist who accepts team effort in the use of the language.

"Why" does such a person write? The answer is: to incorporate formally the observations and conclusions drawn from a professional analysis for those readers responsible for meeting financial and operational standards.

NOTES

[1] Bradford Cadmus, *Operational Auditing Handbook,* Institute of Internal Auditors, Inc., Altamonte Springs, Fla., 1964, p. 31. Copyright 1964 by The Institute of Internal Auditors, Inc. Reprinted by permission of The Institute of Internal Auditors, Inc.

[2] *The New York Times*, Feb. 7, 1971. © 1971 by The New York Times Company. Reprinted by permission.

[3] American Institute of Certified Public Accountants, *Codification of Statements on Auditing Standards*, no. 1 to 26, par. 509.07, pp. 260–261, New York, 1980.

[4] United States General Accounting Office, *Standards for Audit of Governmental Organizations, Programs, Activities, and Functions*, 1981 Revision, Government Printing Office, Washington.

[5] AICPA, *Codification . . .* , par. 517.01, p. 283.

[6] James W. Gunn, "Chief's Corner," *U.S. Army Audit Agency Bulletin*, vol. 465-37, Winter 1971, pp. 6–7.

[7] Department of the Army, Headquarters United States Army Audit Agency, *Circular No. 36-306-1*, 16 June 1975, p. 2.

7 Recognizing recipients

No matter how correctly writers express themselves, the proof of an advisory report lies in its effect upon the readers and their subsequent actions. Writers aim to win agreement and to get management to correct problems. Recognition that a problem exists must be achieved; the best-laid proposals for improvement will go astray unless they are persuasively presented. As the key to a winning report, functional authors adapt their material in preconceived directions. Advance analysis of the readers' receptivity requires perception of individual and organizational needs. "Sensitivity" is one word for this approach; "imagination" is another, imagination in taking into account personal preferences (or prejudices) and responsibilities (or restrictions). Finding the right approach pattern is difficult because the report of an audit (financial or operational), of a consulting engagement, or of an investigation is usually directed to more than one person.

Typically, "runs" of formal reports range from a dozen copies into the hundreds. If there were only one copy, as may be the case for confidential investigations or inspections, the writer could easily form a mental picture of one recipient with particular interests, reservations, and motivations and with a known degree of familiarity with the subject.

POLICY LEVEL

By custom, the finished document is directed to the chief executive officer, the chairman of a board, the commanding officer, or the head of a civilian agency, inasmuch as final acceptance (or rejection) comes from that echelon. Top management itself, whether an individual or a group, bears the responsibility to taxpayers (in the case of public enterprise) or to clients and investors (in the case of private enterprise) for services or profits: "The report should be addressed to the client, or to the board of directors or the stockholders of the client if the appointment is made by them or if such address is preferred."[1]

A high executive group seldom feels its own goals are being realized fully, so such recipients are at one and the same time dubious and hopeful about their best efforts, even apprehensive of too much exposure. Top management remains free to refute an auditor's findings and, of course, frequently does. Even when concurring with criticisms, the managerial officers may reject the auditor's recommendations in favor of their own solutions to problems upon which they themselves reach mutual agreement.

IMPLEMENTATION LEVEL

The actual impact of the findings normally relates to persons at a lower echelon, those who are immediately affected by the specific conditions at the "activity" level. The "doer," versus the policymaker, may be the source from which the auditor or consultant receives the information, or the "doer" may be the cause of the problem. Certainly the implementation or nonimplementation of recommendations devolves upon middle and lower management. Practical effectiveness of a report includes more than those at the top.

When there are only two or three levels of readers, it is still relatively easy to adjust the wording and amount of detail to meet divergent needs. In the long run, the readers extend all the way from top to bottom and all the way from those with biased reactions to those without such reactions. When there are scores and more whose cooperation has to be secured, adaptation taxes the ingenuity of communicators. They will find themselves wishing for a crystal ball at times. ·

PUBLIC INVOLVEMENT

If a report is subject to general release or is found relevant to political or legal proceedings, the audience may include the whole newspaper-reading public. Certified Public Accountant (CPA) firms have become acutely conscious of such an eventuality. At least one federal agency refers in the prefatory pages of its reports to the public information act requiring release of the report to the press:

> In accordance with the principles of the Freedom of Information Act (Public Law 90-23) ... reports issued to the Department's grantees and contractors are made available, if requested, to the press and the general public.

Forewarned of such unrestricted circulation, the author can be forearmed. To take precautions against the possibilities of being quoted out of context, necessary qualifications can be built into statements. One government department was headlined as finding that millions of dollars had been wasted in carrying out a certain program. The figure, if quoted in context, would have been seen to be a projected estimate over a long period. Instead, newspaper readers believed that their hard-earned tax dollars had already been frittered away. After that experience, the agency instructed all its report-writers to identify a projection as such within the same sentence that states the basis for the projection.

Recently, report-writers have become especially conscious of the whole mass of newspaper readers. Journalists' copy about misuse of taxpayers' contributions, excessive political contributions, extravagant expenditure of government appropriations, unethical practices, and mismanagement is often derived from available reports.

Likewise, legally required reports and certifications of private corporations have made the front pages from coast to coast. Language curtailing circulation of financial reports in which clients have imposed restrictions is suggested by the American Institute of Certified Public Accountants (AICPA): "This report is solely for the internal information of the Company's management; it is not to be referred to or presented to anyone outside the Company for any purpose because of the restricted nature of our examination."[2] Efforts to control distribution of such documents are not always successful; therefore, careful drafting is an insurance policy.

RECIPIENTS' CHARACTERISTICS

It is the failure of writers to foresee what they are up against and to write accordingly that dooms the most logical, the most grammatical statements. In attempts to prepare for the diversified readers of analytical reports, the characteristics of those readers may be diagnosed and thus appropriately dealt with.

Is the audit-writer addressing an expert? Auditees are more than just knowledgeable and experienced in their own fields; they are apt to be most highly specialized in those fields. Organizations that warrant (or require) the invested effort of "cradle-to-the-grave" auditing are usually engaged in projects of crucial value to the public or the private sector of the economy or both. Such management teams know their jobs and occupy posts necessitating a high degree of competence. If it is a company that is being scrutinized, it may be the only producer of an indispensable metal or the major manufacturer of an essential product. If it is a government agency, the agency may be the responsible provider of a subsistence program or the unit controlling a particular missile.

Accountants and other analysts have long been aware that they cannot themselves become equally knowledgeable about the specialty they are auditing; they cannot acquire comparable experience in that given subject. By the same token, they have learned not to expect financial expertise on the part of all auditees.

Reports are not addressed to fellow auditors. To execute their own obligations, auditors rely on the standards, tests, procedures, and systems known by them to be applicable to many fields. The tone reflected in a report does not have to call into question the professional competence of the recipient. The recipient must, at the same time, be given confidence in the professional training of the auditor. By demonstrating experience in regard to effectiveness and economy, the auditor can enlist the specialist's respect at the same time that respect is demonstrated for the expert under review.

Can the recipients be regarded as demanding and skeptical? They do indeed demand accuracy with foolproof facts to support any criticism of their operations. If they can find one soft spot in the reasoning or the evidence presented, they incline to reject the results as a whole. One unfounded assumption offers the opportunity the reader may be looking for to throw doubt upon the writer's overall credibility. One unverifiable dollar figure or one unrepresentative example is all it takes (the one "rotten apple"). The reader of any examination is undeniably demanding and skeptical.

Do those on the receiving end constitute a "captive" audience? Largely, yes. Like it or not, an auditee's work is being subjected to the painful process of review by "outsiders." Even the internal auditor is regarded as such. Those audited have no choice; they must receive, read, mark, and inwardly digest the critical findings.

They are certainly not reading for pleasure. No matter what the content, the very act of having to peruse page after page is an ordeal on the job. Because it is time-consuming, it is done as rapidly as possible. Managerial personnel are the victims of what they call "information input overload." Most busy working people would prefer to get it by ear: to answer the phone, talk face-to-face, or participate in a group interchange. But on-the-job writing of any kind is done for one purpose, to be read; it is not done for the pleasure of composition, nor are the addressees free to take it or leave it when the document appears on their desks.

Knowing that a thick-looking report is a drain on time as well as attention, the reader may put off the moment of truth. When that moment arrives and it is time to buckle down and see what is being said in judgment on the best efforts that have been put forth, the reader brings to the task understandable reluctance. Involuntary reading puts the writing itself at an automatic disadvantage as compared with voluntary reading, done by choice and at leisure.

Are the report recipients resistant? Naturally so. To a greater or lesser extent, their defenses are up before the title page is turned. How do writers overcome this handicap? Unless they do, all the facts and all the judgments in the report may be fruitless. One industrial expert made the point a long time ago that: "Communication is not an end in itself, but a means to an end. The over-all purpose of communication is to influence the mind and actions of the receiver, not to get something off the communicator's mind."[3] If the readers can be reassured at the outset, their minds may be partially set at rest, and the resistance level lowered. They usually think that operations for which they and their staffs are responsible have been conducted as well as humanly possible in view of the inevitable limitations managers face over which they have no control. The other possibility is that they know, deep down, their own weaknesses (as well as strengths) and are fearful of disclosure. Either way, they come to the reading with the finger on the trigger. So the writer more often than not is at a disadvantage from the start.

The apprehensiveness associated with the auditor's personal arrival on the scene, which takes place well before the report itself arrives but which is the necessary beginning, is seldom attributable to any sense of guilt on management's part. Wrongdoing (fraud or abuse) is the occasional finding as compared with careless, inadvertent, unintentional, or seemingly inescapable violations of regulations; unprofitable practices; retention of inefficient personnel; or nonproductive activities. Management feels, in the pressure under which it moves today, the near impossibility of complete conformance to its own intentions or fulfillment of its highest objectives. As one repeat audit noted:

> Our prior recommendations were not fully implemented because of the turnover of branch managers.

There are inflexible parameters such as staffing, time, space, and cash that confront the executive. Yet the auditor cannot be expected to make indulgent judgments or condone conditions. The objections found to ongoing operations and the shortcomings in performance may be reported to a higher level or repeated in a follow-up survey.

It is the explanation by the auditor or consultant or inspector of what may already be realized as shortcomings which makes management reluctant to see the problems put in print. Now, however, the audit does not stop at disclosure of negatives; the constructive report seeks actual changes through new methods or through prevention of potential mistakes. So management is beginning to look for the positive as well as the negative in what has to be read.

That report which, by its tone, style, and sequence, emphasizes constructive alternatives decreases the defensiveness of management and increases receptivity to what is being reported. The facts of the findings remain the same; the hoped-for results differ because of the tone in which the findings are presented: "Auditing, by its very nature, has a degree of criticism, but good auditing goes beyond bare criticism; it provides constructive recommendations . . . our assistance . . . can only be effective if our recommendations receive favorable reaction. . . ."[4] As more and more reports are building on the prospects of future accomplishment instead of on pointing the finger of blame for past conditions, the recipients' apprehensions may be replaced by a willingness to listen. That way, the biggest gap of all, the credibility gap, begins to close.

On the brighter side of readers' responses, can the readers be considered open-minded? It seems increasingly likely. How so? Where self-confidence and genuine pride of performance are sufficiently high, responsible management is open to new ideas and new ways to achieve even stronger results. In dispelling negative predisposition to criticism, writers can exercise initiative. They need to allay a fear or an unwarranted sense of guilt that some of the most conscientious managers instinctively feel when confronted with an audit or investigation. Good news presented before the bad serves such a purpose. When the tone is forward-looking, receptivity may replace initial resistance and defensiveness. The reader will then be ready to hear positive options. Such a manager believes in the answer to the old conundrum:

Q. "What is the biggest room in the world?"

A. "The room for improvement."

Even more than being open-minded, the high-level reader, particularly, may be eager to hear new ideas. Such is the desire of private entrepreneurs who, on their own initiative, call in consultants to undertake an overall appraisal of operations. These managers may be seeking diversification, computerization, increased sales, or faster productivity. Such readers, though remaining uncommitted to implementation or proposals that may be made, are looking for what the report has to offer. Alternative recommendations may be welcomed.

Can it be said, even, that management is receptive to criticism? Never say "never." The new boss, like the new broom, may wish to sweep clean. If there are criticisms of what transpired before he or she took charge, it will be no personal reflection. In another sense, responsible officials may be eager to hear from their auditors (preferably their own internal staff) about negative findings likely otherwise to come from outside. It is possible that management itself may propose the areas of examination. Management of this kind often seeks corroboration for the points it wishes to change itself, points which the manager has been trying without success to convey up the line to superiors. An internal audit team may receive requests to review specific activities. In such a fortunate circumstance auditor and auditee come closer without losing their necessarily distinct roles.

Will the recipients be prepared (that is, psychologically ready) for what they have to read? The fact that most of them will already have heard what lies between the covers of the report before it reaches their desks is a plus factor. Contacts by word of mouth begin with the initial, perhaps perfunctory, pleasantries at the time the audit team moves in. Discussion "on site" continues daily with the actual workers and supervisors until the drafted findings are ready for presentation near or at the summit.

During this exit conference management personnel may get some idea of how good or how bad they are going to look in print. Doubtful points may be ironed out, facts may be clarified, and mistaken impressions may be corrected. Neither party professes infallibility. Minor disagreements may be negotiated. The battle line may be drawn, but the other's point of view is heard: "Mission comments were considered prior to issuance of this report" is a frequent statement in military audits. During this oral phase of the reporting process, the recipient becomes preconditioned for the written phase.

FULFILLMENT OF EXPECTATIONS

Within each reader, these characteristics may be found in varying degrees: knowledgeability, skepticism, sense of "captivity," and resistance; all these, but also open-mindedness, eagerness, and hopefulness. The writer's difficulty is not merely that of anticipating the reactions such characteristics produce. The real problem is having to address multiple levels of familiarity and unfamiliarity. As one master communicator says: "It is now necessary to warn the writer that his concern for the reader must be pure: he must sympathize with the reader's plight (most readers are in trouble about half the time) but never seek to know his wants."[5] Much as everyone wants to hear "You're all right," everyone needs to hear weaknesses as well. Sympathy, to use E. B. White's term for the writer-reader relation, cannot be undermined by loss of independence.

Some (those at the top) are presumably conversant with overall administrative needs but not necessarily with technicalities. The person who has to implement a specific recommendation is probably the technician without the broader kind of involvement. How much detail should be included? How much "jargon" (specialized terminology) can safely be used? Such are the questions an auditor has to answer. Some readers' skepticism makes them ready to take offense before they read the first page. Others, feeling they will have to read and "go along" anyway, are impatient and say, "Give it to me straight. Don't play games."

Then there are the cooperative, preconditioned readers for whom directness and objectivity pose no problems. Functional reporters, like other published authors, write to meet diverse needs and interests. If they write well in terms of content, orderliness, and clarity, they overcome the disparateness of readers and bridge the gap that otherwise produces confusion and antagonism.

Among the techniques of tonal adaptation are a constructive vocabulary and depersonalization of criticism. Attribution of credit where credit is due is possible. An internal audit of an educational institution's department of student accounting contained the statement:

> As suggested by Student Accounting, we recommend that monthly processing of the student accounts be controlled by the student accounts office.

Recognition of pluses as well as minuses motivates readers by showing them how to achieve their own goals. All such resources as arrangement of sequence and "clean" format are needed because of the relationship between sender and receiver. The auditors may merely suggest and advise; it is not their prerogative to command, to order, or to direct.

The "selling" of a message is incumbent upon the auditors just as management consultants know it is incumbent upon them. They may recommend, and nothing more. How, then, to avoid sounding like an accuser or a scold? The stakes are high. The operational auditor, by assisting management in reaching its own objectives, produces a winning report. Management objectives range from meeting a specified profit level to product development; from market penetration to fulfillment of public obligation; from reduction of cost to introduction of social programs. Reports that help top management and are therefore well received at that level may still be critical of lower levels and therefore antagonize lower-level personnel. Such a dilemma must be avoided.

Gaps in the communication process beset every functional writer today: There are differences in objectives, education, economic status, generation, national origin, sex, race, religion, rank, or organizational status. The gaps that are obvious, such as language or geography, are the ones most easily overcome. It is the unseen dividing lines that put writers at cross-purposes with their readers. The dimension of distance that keeps sender and receiver apart is not always measurable on a yardstick or even visible to the naked eye.

Probably the greatest obstacle for communicators is the obligatory difference between their professional roles and those of their readers:

the critic versus the performer. Till this separation is surmounted, attack and defense are the name of the game. In a different context, Churchill said of his opposition: " . . . adversary relation is also undeniable and indispensable. . . . We should be grateful for this opposition. They help us improve our own performance."[6]

That being the case, whoever is writing must safeguard whatever is being written to whoever will be reading it. Defensiveness is the natural stance of the "doers," whether they are or are not proud of their performance. The figure of speech about "couching" one's word to avoid misinterpretation can be taken almost literally. Writer and reader both have the instinct for self-protection. The former is obliged to detect and disclose signs of failure of a "mission." The latter is the one who will determine ultimate success.

COMMUNICATION GAPS

In the operational audit's short history, developments have been moving fast to resolve the inherent tensions between writer and reader. The communication process is where the resolution will make itself apparent. An audit, whether financial or operational, is conceived today as an instrument to help management without sacrificing independence of view or assuming responsibility for what happens. Constructiveness as opposed to destructiveness is an interpersonal language and an interorganizational language among truly professional people.

There is not much need for the writer to worry about the reader who sees the common objectives. Nor is the struggle insurmountable if other problems inherent in the multiplicity of levels are properly addressed. The real danger to the writer comes from that one, single, unanticipated reader who has, nevertheless, legitimate access to the report. Given an awareness and appreciation of the audience, writers must take only one last step, often an act of the imagination, and ask themselves: Who is my single most difficult reader? The answer is likely to be: the reader I forgot.

To "whom" is the report addressed? The answer is: a many-headed tiger.

"Where" is this multiple readership located? How far is it from the originator? The answer is: a long way. However, the gap must be closed by the report process.

NOTES

[1] American Institute of Certified Public Accountants, *Statement on Auditing Standards*, no. 1, par. 511.05, New York, 1973, p. 81.

[2] AICPA, *Statement on Auditing Standards*, par. 515.04a, p. 85.

[3] Keith Davis, *What You Should Know about Administrative Communication*, Indiana University, Bureau of Business Research, Bloomington, March 1954, p. 2.

[4] James W. Gunn, "Chief's Corner," *U.S. Army Audit Agency Bulletin*, vol. 465-37, Winter 1971, pp. 6–7.

[5] William Strunk, Jr., and E. B. White, *The Elements of Style*, 2d ed., The Macmillan Company, New York, 1972, p. 77.

[6] Quoted in *The New York Times*, Dec. 10, 1976. © 1976 by The New York Times Company. Reprinted by permission.

8 Sequencing coverage

The report of a financial, operational, or management audit has to be organized in terms of its situational controls. Merriam-Webster's *Third New International Dictionary* (unabridged) defines "situation" in this way: "Position with respect to conditions and circumstances." As related to workaday communication, the definition may be interpreted to mean the factors and forces surrounding and controlling the outcome of a transaction that has to be reported.

"Who" is writing to "whom," "wherever" the recipient may be? The reason for such an audit, the "why" of it, is usually understood by the two control points, the "who" and the "whom"; the reason is to identify defects and to facilitate such changes as may be proved necessary. The pacing and timing of input is another of the situational determinants: the "when" factor.

With the relevant situational factors clearly in mind, it becomes easier to put first things first. The timing of the "bytes" of input to the human mind is as essential as the programming of a computer. Readers want the necessary pieces of information as they go along; they do not want to be made to wait or to skip ahead. It is not good enough for a writer to say to a questioning reader, "Wait, I'm going to get to that point. You'll find the answer later." Without the calculated determination of "when" a point should be delivered, matters of primary significance may be buried or lost. Establishment of the order of importance has to be based upon the writer's purposes and the

117

readers' needs. In that way, the two essentials of good organization, unity and emphasis, can be achieved. Logic and psychology, which are the two hard taskmasters of any practical writer, will then be served.

UNITY AND EMPHASIS

Out of the entire report must come an integrated impression, not a welter of uncorrelated items. A report is not meant to be a guessing game but rather a document with a well-connected series of conditions and potential actions. If the developmental stages are logically and psychologically timed in the presentation, the result is concurrence and the desired consequence (in the literal sense of that word). There is a "flow," and, like the flow of a river, it will move irresistibly from source to outlet. If the reader gets a churning mass of unsupported opinions or unfocused details, no conclusive result is reached.

Although coverage should be unified, certain points take priority over others; the reader is not going to give equal attention to all. The major matters must be determined in advance if they are to be transmitted as such with the priority they deserve. The writer, not the reader, must make that determination.

According to the old "common law" of human behavior, emphasis belongs to the first and last positions. That is why the reader-in-a-hurry skims by jumping from beginning to end. What stands in between is the filling. So fundamental is the psychologists' law of primacy that it governs the use of the opening position of most practical communications (a letter or a memo, for instance, as well as a formal report).

Within a report, the principle applies overall. Emphasis falls not only upon the first and last pages of the total document but also upon the first and last parts of each separate finding as a subunit.

CHOICE OF PATTERN

In sequencing a report, apart from the presence or absence of a separate synopsis, the first thing to decide is whether to include the key point or points in the introductory pages. Key points may be considered the auditor's chief results, consisting of overall problems, proposed solutions, or both. Without delay, a consultant usually puts a finger upon the underlying source of a company's effectiveness or ineffectiveness. Such material belongs first or last for the sake of emphasis, not in the middle. Contributing factors come in between. The choice the writer has to make is between the direct approach and the indirect approach.

Direct approach

If the key point is regarded as the general judgment which an auditor is going to express, a different impact will be produced depending upon where that judgment stands. To be direct, it must appear somewhere in the opening pages, as near the beginning as possible. To present directly does not mean jumping to conclusions. The thinking process must be indirect if it is to be sound and fair. Once, however, the thought has led the writer to a determination, that conclusion may be presented first instead of last.

In one long report, the first paragraph contained the comprehensive judgment:

> Procurement activities at the XYZ site are now completed. Although some administrative phases of the procurement processes are in compliance with applicable regulations, the actions taken generally were not effective in supplying essential equipment.

In an even more direct approach, the chief matter of emphasis would be contained in the very first sentence, not the second. One decisive sentence standing first is capable of fast communication:

> Our examination disclosed that the borrower had not deposited fully the amount of sales proceeds generated from the XYZ loans as required by the pertinent loan agreement.

Some readers, and there are more and more of them, grow impatient for the immediate "answer" as their time for reading runs out. The trend toward directness in presentation is on the rise, even though the nature of the key point in auditing is apt to be negative. Those on the receiving end expect as much; they are preconditioned for critical analysis and are looking for the judgments which they know are there somewhere. They do not want to search the haystack for the needle.

The decision between directness and indirectness must be made even more carefully with regard to each finding within the document. The separate sections may follow one pattern or the other, but consistency helps the reader. What is most expeditious is for the report as a whole and for each section to be on the same wavelength from start to finish.

At the level of the individual finding, within the body of the report, directness is demonstrated in this opening sentence:

> Because of an apparent oversight, ABC overstated its March claims for predetermination.

In its initial phrase, the wording of this quick confrontation also shows some consideration for the reader's reaction.

One federal agency made a break with its own past in deciding to put the recommendation itself almost (not quite) at the very beginning of each finding. The practice had been to place the recommendation last, at the end of each section. The objective in the changeover was twofold: (1) to permit fast intake and (2) to stress a positive tone at the outset. A recommendation by its very nature is more affirmatively worded than the statement of the problem. So the older format used in the agency's findings was revised to appear in this new way:

Finding: Record-keeping Responsibility

Condition

Geographical dispersion of officials charged with maintaining weekly records prevented timely and complete flow of information.

Recommendation

Office locations of those responsible for weekly reports should be reassigned to facilitate prompt and inclusive distribution of essential data.

Not only is this sequence direct, but in presenting the recommendation no later than the second paragraph, the emphasis is shifted from the existing difficulty to the positive potentiality. The development, supporting the negative factor, comes later.

If the key point indicates the plus as well as the minus aspects of the findings, the reader may be better able to accept the fast confrontation. Direct presentation of one condition in a school began like this:

> The institution, thus far underequipped for safety, should buy flameproof curtains and have them cleaned outside the institution.

Not only is the criticism stated (the need for the protective curtains), but in addition the recommendation is made for their purchase and care. The condition and the cure have been conveyed in one sentence. Another direct start was this:

> Unexpended funds were not made available to the manpower pool.

This condition is set forth without its cure. It is undeniably direct (though not positive) because the specific defect has been disclosed. The negative status has not been offset by a constructive turn. The tone that is set is, as a consequence, flatly critical. The contrasting tone can be further illustrated:

> The XYZ process, if effectively implemented, should provide local management with data useful in performance evaluation, production control, and resource planning.

Regardless of tone, directness is becoming more and more frequent; the assumption is that most recipients expect an audit report to be more unfavorable than favorable, so why wait? But there is an option, as always in the communication process. A decision in favor of direct presentation must be weighed against the alternative values of indirect presentation.

Indirect approach

There are contrasting advantages to the indirect sequence. If the overall judgment is withheld until the details of the report have been unfolded, the writer gains time to build the evidence. One long report began:

AUDIT REPORT

INTRODUCTION
XYZ administers numerous discretionary grant programs to individuals, nonprofit organizations, and educational enterprises for research and training. At the time of our review, XYZ administered about forty discretionary grant programs. Awards made or continued during fiscal years 1982 and 1983 by XYZ amounted to about 4,300 and had an estimated value of $209 million.

Nothing has been revealed anywhere in the introduction as to the adequacy or inadequacy of the administration of the number of awards or of the amounts. From here on, the writer can lead the reader to what may seem inevitably, by the time the close comes, to be an unfavorable conclusion or, conceivably, to one that is partly unfavorable and partly favorable. This is what one reader regarded as a process of self-conviction ("self-incrimination" was the exact word used). It is true that what readers can be brought to see for themselves they believe more readily, though this is not the only way to persuade.

In the same report as that quoted, each finding began in a similar, indirect way, so that the inductive process remained consistent:

FINDING 9

General administrative expenses are required by a standing rule to be adjusted when a redistribution can be made by assignment of a cost grouping directly to the area benefited.

It remains to be proved whether the "standing rule" was observed or violated. The facts, if left to speak for themselves, can do just that before the writer delivers the final determination. Investigators should do just that: let the facts speak for themselves. Likewise, if auditors decide that a report's findings are likely to be disputed, by and large, the purpose may be better served as Francis Bacon, always the pragmatist, suggested: "It is better to sound [that is, to sound out] a person with whom one deals afar off, than to fall upon the point at first...."[1]

The best use of indirectness demonstrates a gradual process of building mutual agreement as to the obvious steps to be taken. Many audit reports have traditionally been presented indirectly on the grounds of persuasiveness. If a report of any kind is critical, management's predisposition to self-defense may lead the critic to make a cautious, exploratory approach.

Time pressures now being felt by all on-the-job readers are leading writers to be more direct. The fact that a client knows in advance that changes are going to be suggested is a strong argument for directness. The overburdened reader may welcome the quick diagnosis (the "condition") at the outset; the diagnosis may be offset if the recommendation (the "cure") is also given at the start. A trend toward the direct sequence in consulting, reviewing, and auditing presentations is definitely noticeable.

COMPONENTS FOR INTRODUCTIONS

There are certain introductory components on which every reader relies for an easy start. These components can be adjusted to accord with a direct or an indirect method. Regardless of the timing of the confrontation (the "when" factor), it is possible to identify those components which are suitable for the beginning of a report as a whole. The components are the same within the report for the beginnings of findings or sections (the internal introductions). Basically, there are five components if the key point is included for the sake of directness. Otherwise there are four:

Identification of subject

Statement of purpose

Inclusion of background and scope

Indication of key point (optional)

Plan of presentation.

Such elements are easily recognized, often being grouped under the heading "Introduction," but they are identifiable even without that clue. The exact order of the five points, as illustrated, is subject to rearrangement:

Subject	(1)	We made an audit of the Health Center of the Metropolitan District.
Purpose	(2)	The special review was undertaken at the request of the Medical Officer in charge of the district.
Background and scope	(3a)	Although the Health Center opened in 1981, its activities were not required to be extended over the entire metropolitan area until January 1, 1983.
	(3b)	Accordingly, our examination covered calendar year January 1 through December 31, 1983.
Key point	(4)	Inability to fill the vacancies with qualified medical staff prevented the Health Center from rendering certain services to patients entitled to receive them.
Plan of presentation	(5)	The Health Center's services primarily affected were prenatal care, public education, and immunization.

Such fivefold introductory material may be lengthened or shortened, depending upon relevant factors like the presence or absence of a preceding synopsis or the length of the total document. The five items may be differently sequenced in relationship to one another so that the key point gets delivered even sooner. Sometimes the introduction itself becomes the synopsis. The advantage then is simplification of format, brevity, and avoidance of repetition. The disadvantage is that the readers may not realize, without the guidance of a separate heading, that they are indeed getting a summary.

In report openings, the identification of the subject is seldom missing (sentence 1 in the model). Identification of the purpose is equally clear as quoted (sentence 2). Background in general (sentence 3a) needs to be held down as to extent in view of professional hyperconscientiousness in giving the full, researched rundown of financial, descriptive, historical, or regulatory aspects. Often an excess of such material slows up the readers who, not yet motivated to take in all the background, have no peg on which to hang it. Some explanatory items should be weeded out and used later in correlation with the specific condition needing that empirical support.

Scope, on the other hand, can be and usually is quickly defined (sentence 3b) in all audits, inspections, and consultation engagements.

In the introduction as modeled, directness is demonstrated by the presence of the key point (sentence 4). It would be possible to omit that key point and have a clear, efficient, but indirect beginning. (The omitted statement would then be reserved for the other position of emphasis, the end.) Here, the model as given is fairly direct. The initial phrase in the key point of the introduction ("Inability to fill the vacancies") constitutes the cause which explains, if it does not excuse, the inadequacy of services (to be specified later). The paragraph could be made even more direct if sentence 4 were reworded and placed first in the paragraph.

To give a plan of presentation (sentence 5) is to give specific information on how the reader is to find the pathway through what follows. The reader should expect to see particular findings in the order specified in the model: (1) prenatal care, (2) public health education, and (3) immunization. Such a technique can easily be mastered, once its helpfulness to the reader is understood. The technique is equally valuable in the opening of a report and in the openings of the subsequent findings.

As an illustration of how to use a plan of presentation at the level of the *first* finding, the finding's own internal introduction would contain a sentence such as:

> ... In view of limited staff available, no home visits were made, clinic hours were held in the morning only, and instructional pamphlets were not distributed.

The sequential series of points announced for the initial finding serves as its own self-evident plan of presentation for that finding. The items in such a series may be preceded by small Roman numerals if they are complicated enough to require such separation within the sentence.

There is no question as to where, within an introduction, such advance notice of the developmental plan should stand: last. By placing it at the introduction's end (as in the model), transition is naturally provided into the midsection itself. Such a statement serves as a natural carry-over.

Only one caution is needed regarding the style of a plan of presentation. It may be worded so mechanically that the readers feel they are being insulted or told the obvious. An undesirable, mechanical way of restating the plan of presentation just offered as an illustration for the finding would be:

> It will be shown that the staff was limited in number. Then the unfavorable results will be demonstrated.

Possibly less distasteful to readers but still mechanical is the sort of standardized wording to be found at the end of Part I (the introduction) of many audit reports:

Part I consists of the general coverage of the audit. Part II presents individual conditions and recommendations. Part III contains history and applicable regulations.

The frequency of such obvious wording makes it easy to illustrate:

The recommendations are stated in the same sequence as the Findings and Observations in Section V, above, in order to facilitate access thereto.

This is better than no advance notice, to be sure. Mechanical wording, such as that shown, is routine and transferable from one report to another. More helpful plans of presentation are individualized to prepare the reader substantively for what lies ahead.

MASTER PLANS FOR MIDSECTIONS

The extent of detail required to support the key point or points of an audit varies. The more extensive the report, the more problematic is its development. The reader needs an easy-to-follow pathway between the beginning and the end of the document as a whole. The same need relates to the midsection of each finding itself (that is, the sequence of details between each finding's introduction and conclusion).

What makes a sequence easy to follow? The first answer that comes to mind is: logic. But what makes an arrangement logical? Rationality. The question as to what is rational may be answered: that which is reasonable. And what seems reasonable?

Familiarity is the real answer in deciding whether the path provided for a reader through the detailed midsection will seem logical, rational, or reasonable. The study of reports of all kinds in the working world, audits included, suggests that there are at least five master plans for the arrangement of midsection material:

Chronological (time)

Spatial (location)

Functional (aspect)

Comparative (pro and con)

Ranking (priority)

These patterns, whether perceived by such names or not, are all utilized instinctively by seasoned writers. They may be used separately or in combination.

The very frequency with which such master patterns can be detected means that they are not original, in the sense that a novel by Ernest Hemingway tracks unknown territory. Each work by such an author is a unique creation in concept, style, and organization. There is no well-traveled road through the dark woods. Persistent readers may keep trying, reading and rereading, till they find the way and reach the richly rewarding destination.

No such effort or motivation to find their own way through a jungle of detail can be expected of report readers. They need to be led by the hand along an accustomed road to the end of the journey without losing their way. Replacing the analogy of the road by an analogy of a river, the report should have that often-expressed objective of "flow." Most reports that do flow follow one or more of a few well-worn channels.

Chronological

The sense of time is fundamental to human interaction. Stonehenge is believed to be a primitive calendar of sorts. The Western world has become bound to the wheel of the clock. Not only are wristwatches worn; miniature calendars are carried as well by many who depend on them in their professional and social lives. (Watches often include calendars and alarms.) Children, even babies, live by intervals to which they are conditioned by hunger or waking. The chronological sequence underlies many children's stories, "Cinderella," for instance.

Because awareness of the hours of the day, the days of the month, and the months of the year is second nature to reader and writer alike, intricate detail is simplified by chronological development. It was Einstein who wrote: "The psychological subjective feeling of time enables us to order our impressions, to state that one event precedes another."[2] Development based on time is objective in that no point can safely be ignored. Investigators' most frequent sequence is by order of dates or even hours. Straight chronology is the least subjective method of presentation.

If emphasis on one special period is desired, a variant of the chronological method can be used: the flashback. Here, the climax of the problem is made known before the events leading up to, and coming after, the circumstances.

Chronology underlies every audit report in the designation by exact dates of the period covered. Pertinent, also, is the auditor's sense of time in the old adage of the profession: "Report facts in the past tense." (The cutoff date will have been passed before the report is distributed.)

Spatial

Another dimension besides time is inherent to the logic of communication: spatial arrangement. People are accustomed, for instance, to getting their bearings geographically. Knowing the points of the compass is as basic as knowing the figures on the clock face. Companies and agencies themselves are structured by districts, regions, continents, or countries.

Just as chronology is objective, so is location. It is expected that a report which is sectioned by sites will make orderly reference to all considered within the scope. The auditor cannot, without explaining, choose to ignore one such site.

Time and space are the two most basic and objective methods of guiding a reader. Though naturally used in such documents as audit programs, trip reports, inspection visits, procedures, progress reports, and investigations, these patterns may not serve some of the more involved subjects.

Functional

The functional sequence constitutes the most frequent means for dealing with selected aspects of an operation. "Function" refers to that aspect or activity of an ongoing process or program chosen for discussion. In reports of audit and consultation engagements, as in management reports in general, the functional outline is the most frequent. Financial audits often use the standard, comparative headings of a balance sheet itself, like "Assets" and "Liabilities." Within this breakdown may be functional subheadings such as "Utility Plant Investments" and "Cash Transactions."

Headings are the readers' guideposts along whatever pathway they are to follow. In one military audit of a service club, the set of headings clearly illustrated a functional coverage:

1. Bar Operation
2. Mess Operation
3. Slot Machine Activity
4. Payroll System
5. Cash Controls

This outlines the reporting of particular aspects of the service club which required comment. In that not every aspect of the program or entity may have to be included, functional reporting is subjective. Readers need to be given confidence that those topics mentioned are all that are necessary, that the topics not presented are not significant.

The functional approach, which is actually the predominant method, is especially contributive and helpful. When it comes to getting corrective action and to holding down length, subjectivity (selectivity) versus objectivity (all-inclusiveness) may be the most serviceable approach.

Comparative

Inclusion of both strengths and weaknesses in discussing a subject means balanced reporting. The comparative system, as such, implies identifying the pros as well as the cons of a condition. To rely on comparison as the primary sequence would mean use of top-level headings representing both the negative and the positive findings. Occasionally, but not often, an audit report does so:

Proper Control of Cash

Inadequacy of Stockage

Overdue Progress Reports

Accuracy of Budget Forecast

The comparative sequence is less characteristic of an audit report than of other types like progress reports. There, it is customary to give a reader first, under one heading, what has been accomplished as planned and then, under another heading, what tasks have fallen behind schedule.

An auditor can still make a balanced presentation without giving the comparison of pluses and minuses the chief emphasis. Balanced reporting versus exception reporting is spreading widely.

Ranking

Because of instinct, precedent, or training, in some mysterious way auditors in general, whether financial or operational, arrange the series of findings in a report in one prevailing pattern. The most significant finding comes first. That is the system of rank ordering.

As an automatic way of arranging findings, it is quick and usually obvious to the writer. Readers who are unfamiliar with operational reports may not realize, however, that they are being given the most important condition first, and the least important last. With financial audits, the dollar sign signals the amounts at stake. In a list of headings from one operational audit, nothing gives notice that item 1 is more in need of correction than item 2, that item 2 is more in need of correction than item 3, and so on:

1. Deposit Procedure
2. Direct Shipment
3. Central Management
4. Disposition of Excess Material
5. Storage of Supplies

The headings from another audit, on the other hand, leave no doubt about the order of presentation (that is, the ranking order):

Travel Allotments ($16,816 overdrawn)

Advances ($8,510 unauthorized)

Petty Cash ($2,015 undeposited)

Long-Distance Calling ($203 untraceable)

Priority remains helpful as an accepted, standard solution that saves the writer's time. It will save time only insofar as the order of materiality remains as clear-cut in operational findings as it has been in financial exceptions. It may become wise to make the recipient aware that priority is implicit.

If the succession of findings in the body of a report follows a rank order, it is natural to present the details within each of the findings also in the order of their importance. Once familiarity with the chosen pattern is achieved, the reader can stay on course easily.

Combinations

Although five particular master patterns have been traced throughout thousands of reports in government and industry, many a successful report is built on the correlation of two or more of these patterns.

To explain: Headings at the first level may be (and usually are) functional, like those already quoted, beginning with:

Bar Operation

At the secondary level, under "Bar Operation," the spatial approach may be introduced:

Operations Review
1. Bar Operation
    a. Counter Attendants
    b. Table Service

The reader is now conditioned for a functional division plus spatial subdivisions throughout:

2. Mess Operation
    a. Kitchen
    b. Dining Hall

   3. Slot Machine Activity

     a. Lobby

     b. Lounge

   4. Payroll System

     a. Office

     b. Cashier's Window

   5. Cash Controls

     a. Accounts Department

     b. Front Desk

Though headings seldom reflect absolute consistency, consistency is a theory to be applied insofar as the subject matter permits. No subject should be distorted for the sake of a theoretical outline. For instance, it is not a problem to have subdivisions for some major headings and not for others. But a general proportioning is expected. As the philosopher-poet Samuel Taylor Coleridge wrote: "Excess in methodizing is opposed to the accumulation of fresh material of thought."[3]

By outlining, even chaotic data may be reduced to some semblance of order. The author, by trying to fit details into a chronological, spatial, functional, comparative, or rank order, will find the easiest path along which to guide the reader. Once undertaken, the interweaving of two or more of the master patterns needs to be maintained with regularity. Both reader and writer then arrive at the same destination, whether it be a short or a long run.

COMPONENTS FOR ENDINGS

The end section of a whole report, like that of a finding within the report, is comparable in emphasis to the beginning section. Such being the case, elements to be considered for inclusion in this strategic spot are:

Summary

Conclusion

Recommendations

Specification of Action

Motivation of Action

Some or all of these five components are worth leaving as the final emphasis in the reader's mind. At the end of most individual findings, these elements are given coverage, although the closing pages of the report as a whole (that is, whatever immediately precedes any appended material) are another matter.

It would be possible to include all five components on one final page of a total report in this fashion:

Summary	(1) Our review covered work orders, parts requests, and individual work hours as related to the quota of vehicles produced in the last quarter of 1982.
Conclusion	(2) Inability to meet the quota was attributable, in our view, to delays, shortages, and lack of available personnel in each of the three aspects examined.
Recommendations	(3) Our recommendations specify earlier deadlines for work orders, initial and periodic parts inventories, and advance estimation of individual work hours.
Specification of Action	(4) To implement the changes needed, revision of existing procedures can be requested by the Projects Chairman.
Motivation of Action	(5) Once it is possible to meet the quarterly quotas of vehicles, the annual production rate will be attainable.

To summarize is not necessarily to repeat. Though the facts being recalled refer back to those already conveyed in the midsection, the "recall" must be highly selective. Unless the reader is reminded of the breadth of information in all the findings, the one single finding presented last receives the major emphasis, and that is not the desired overall impact. The array of all the points, from first to last, may be visualized as so many iron filings strewn upon a flat surface. The summary acts as the magnet that draws the filings into a pattern. Now the reader sees (sentence 1 in the model) the clustering effect that shows how the material took a definite direction.

If the summarizing is written without repeating the exact wording used earlier, the result is one of reinforcement. Verbatim repetition is insulting and not reinforcing. So success depends on style as well as selectivity in the recall.

If the end is to be strengthened, mere summary is not enough; there is more to do than just adding up data. An audit is an analytical message. The next logical step is to draw from the "evidence" a conclusion. This means expressing the opinion, the conclusive judgment, that emerges from the array of factual evidence (sentence 2).

In the ending, the reader needs a signal that more than fact is being indicated, that certain inferences are now being drawn. The ethical aspect of the communication process is preserved by such signaling words as "in our view," which put readers on notice that they have moved into the realm of honest speculation. Though the factual summary should not be open to question, it is the conclusion or conclusions that may be accepted or rejected.

Recommendations logically follow on the heels of the auditor's judgments (sentence 3). They can be spelled out in detail, or they can be rolled up into one generalized proposal for change. Interestingly enough, recommendations appear easier to write than other portions, perhaps because they are positive in nature.

Occasionally, an audit report containing several findings will save all the recommendations till the grand finale. More typically, the end of each finding carries its own recommendation. For instance, sentence 3 in the model could be the capsule version of three separate recommendations that have already been stated at the end of each finding:

Finding 1	Deadlines for the receipt of work orders should be moved from 1 week before commencement of the project to 2 weeks.
Finding 2	Inventories should be taken of the supplies for all standard and nonstandard parts upon initial stockage and at regular intervals thereafter.
Finding 3	Requisite work hours should be estimated for each project as quickly as possible after receipt of a work order.

Having gone this far in giving conclusions, either individually or at the end of the report (preferably in both places), there are two further possibilities if the particular report warrants it. Both these possibilities are in the nature of increasing persuasiveness.

The action needed to carry out the recommendations may be specified: Who is to do what (sentence 4)? Action to effectuate the desired result should sound simple and definite, not vague and wide open, as in this poor example:

> It is probable that, in given circumstances, different responsible parties exercising high-level supervisory powers may wish to consider altering, amending, or deleting present practices in favor of new ones.

The correct approach here would be to open the barn door just wide enough, but not so wide as to leave uncertain options that require more effort than the reader is willing to exert in deciding which way to proceed. The necessary step may be specified:

> We recommend that a provisional indirect cost ratio of 31.5 percent applicable to total direct costs, exclusive of any extraordinary or distorting items such as equipment and library acquisitions, be approved for use by XYZ.

As one last step, action indicated can be accompanied with motivation. What will be the "reward" from proceeding as advised (sentence 5)? The reader can be presented with a picture of what both the adviser and the advised agree must be accomplished. It may be risky to promise dollar savings, and it may be unwise to commit oneself to assured results, but the readers will be more inclined to act promptly and decisively if shown what they can achieve.

OVERALL

With the abstract theory of sequence in mind, the principles of unity and emphasis can be incorporated in an auditor's or consultant's report as a whole or in any section within the total document.

The all-important opening of a report is usually well built, containing four or five of the theoretical components (identification of subject, purpose, background and scope, plan of presentation, and sometimes the major opinion or key point). As one variant seen in many standardized reports, background or scope may be removed to the end as appended material. The thinking is that the auditees themselves know full well the description of their location, size, objective, and so on. The opening is thus accelerated, and other recipients of the report who are less familiar with the situation can find such explanatory details in the appendix.

At the finding level, the introductory components are equally well incorporated. The majority of report-writers are moving toward directness, with the condition (often accompanied by the proposed correction) stated in one or two short opening sentences. This shift toward deductive presentation is gaining ground.

After the formalized introduction, the series of findings constituting the midsection of the report usually follows the pattern of priority, with the most significant condition coming first. However, if the report is directed to two or more officials, each located separately or each differentiated functionally from the other, the findings may be grouped in two or more segments. Then the spatial or functional master patterns form the primary division.

Within each finding the sequencing of the details varies. Often the problem is unfolded chronologically; at other times, comparatively, with the strong and weak aspects balanced against each other.

Less structural strength is typical of the final pages of a report to management than of the first pages. Apart from appended material, if any, the report may stop with the last finding. Auditors, like other authors, are pressed for time at this stage of their task. They may be tired or fearful of excessive repetition. It is not repetition which is needed at the end so much as reinforcement. Each time the problem is mentioned, there should be incremental development, leading to solution. Francis Bacon, in his Elizabethan English, put it like this: "Iterations are commonly loss of time. But there is no such gain of time as to iterate often the state of the question...."[4] By the time the end comes, the reader as well as the writer may be tired; what is wanted is a quick wrap-up emphasizing again ("iteration") the problem ("the state of the question") propounded at the outset but now in its final state.

At the end of a finding itself, emphasis is much more apparent. Most often, the specific recommendation stands last, even though the finding's first paragraph may already have hinted clearly at the coming cure as well as the condition.

Whether an auditor or consultant is using the direct or the indirect method of presentation in a report, reiteration of the key point or points should be left as the last thing in the reader's mind. From a surprising source comes a point for auditors:

> What we call the beginning is often the end
> And to make an end is to make a beginning.
> The end is where we start from....[5]

Good thinking makes good writing come full circle.

Significance of the details, not the details themselves, is what counts. A sense of unity as well as emphasis is conducive to quick and effective action. Sequence depends upon a sense of timing, which itself arises from perception of the reporting situation. The question of "when" to deliver the various components contained in a report has to be answered in terms of the readers' readiness. Important as the detailed midsection of a report is, the writer has to utilize the beginning and the end for their full worth.

NOTES

[1] C. S. Northrup (ed.), *The Essays of Francis Bacon*, Houghton Mifflin Company, Boston, 1908, p. 149.

[2] Albert Einstein and Leopold Infeld, *The Evolution of Physics*, Simon & Schuster, Inc., New York, 1967, p. 295.

[3] S. T. Coleridge, *A Dissertation on the Science of Method*, Charles Griffin & Company, Ltd., London, undated, p. iv.

[4] Northrup, *Essays*, p. 78.

[5] T. S. Eliot, "Little Gidding," *Four Quartets*, in *The Complete Poems and Plays: 1909–1950*, Harcourt Brace Jovanovich, Inc., New York, 1952. p. 144.

9 Designing format

A formal report should be recognized at first glance as distinct from a letter report; an operations audit program must be distinguishable on the surface from a procedures manual; a proposal for an engagement must not resemble the finished documentation of the engagement. Format is the first signal to a reader of what lies ahead. In a particular agency, for instance, the audits of army officers' clubs (being a "nonappropriated" fund activity) are bound in gray over white pages. The same agency publishes its other reports between green covers. "Repeat" recipients know from the color what lies in their in-baskets. In a large manufacturing company, blue paper is used for internal communications coming from the level of a vice-president. The General Accounting Office (GAO) of the federal government publishes in covers of a certain color reports to be released only by congressional committees, whereas another color is used for the reports which the GAO releases itself. Such matters can be standardized for the sake of rapid recognition.

FLEXIBILITY AND FAMILIARITY

Flexibility combined with familiarity is ideal in planning the format of a report. Each kind of communication must show, by its appearance, what it is or is not. Format makes each type of document look, on the surface, like what it is.

For new writers on the staff of an organization, a manual standardizing format is a safeguard and a time-saver. Their readers might otherwise face a muddled mass of material. Familiarity facilitates both the "who" (the person doing the writing) and the "whom" (the person being addressed). Certain prescribed parts are sure to be included, and to be included in a customary arrangement. As one industrial writer explained: "A standardized reporting system reduces the need to worry about how to show the material and allows greater opportunity to worry about what the information says."

Advantageous as traditional presentations may be, there is always the possibility that a particular subject may not fit the mold. If a manual lays down too many minutiae, the innovative author then suffers from the inflexibility. Subjects differ; readers vary; format gets out of date. Situations, unforeseen at the time a manual is prepared, arise, and the treatment calls for departure from the regular pattern.

Good guidelines do permit variation. The challenge becomes one of adaptation for the sake of the writer's purposes and the reader's needs. Modifications can tailor-make a product. Whereas it is easier simply to take the model that worked the last time, the effect may have less impact regarding current conditions. Creativity is riskier than conformity, but within the bounds of acceptability creativity carries special appeal.

Whether the format to be followed is hard and fast or permits timely deviation, certain regular parts are expected in presenting most audits and comparable reviews.

COVER

If it is true that first impressions last longest, the cover of a report is valuable. For instance, the partner in charge of consulting services in an office of one major certified public accounting firm explained that: "... we use a variety of covers depending upon the nature of the engagement. When we believe that our report will receive wide distribution, including other than client personnel, we normally use a more impressive cover...." The outer "wrapping" is the first layer of the communication process. On such matters, individual writers may have little or no choice, merely waiting to see their painstakingly penned statements come forth in the green, blue, brown, black, maroon, buff, or other color which the parent organization has made traditional. A preprinted stock is often kept on hand. A window, cut out in the cover to show the title from the title page itself, is an economy. Once seen in this familiar protective coating, the write-up takes on a kind of dignity; circulation of the finished product without covers is the practice for internal consumption.

Eye appeal, in this graphically oriented age, involves configuration as well as color. Whether the layout is symmetrical or asymmetrical,

Seal of the U.S. Department of Labor. It consists of:
"An anvil, representing industry; a pulley, lever, and
inclined plane, to represent the principles of mechanics; and a plow, representing agriculture. There
is also an eagle with wings spread." (*John W. Leslie,
Department of Labor, letter to author, Mar. 27, 1975.*)

traditional or contemporary, it "says" something about the image of
the issuing source. A simple, striking appearance notifies the reader
that the message is important and that it is coming from an established and authoritative source.

Government groups like business firms are apt nowadays to carry
their own logotypes or emblems (such as the Department of Labor seal
shown) symbolizing their origins.[1]

When it comes to private corporations, the symbolic medium is also
used. Some firms adopt stylized monograms, medieval symbols, or
abstract shapes (such as that of an enzyme, used by one large
pharmaceutical producer). One automotive company is represented
by a familiar oval containing its name in the good old Palmer method
script. The idea behind such devices is not that the initial look should
be lavish or extreme but, rather, that it should appear economical; not
spectacular but recognizable. Communication really reaches down to
the near-subliminal level.

Use of as few words as possible on this outer surface seems best, the
point being to attract attention but not delay the reader. Those few
words, however, have the obligation to identify the document's title,
purpose (like "Report of Audit," "Report to Management," or "Review
of XYZ"), source (name of the issuing group, seldom an individual's
name), place (city or site), and date of publication. Other items may
include a reference number and the name and capacity of the
recipient or group to whom the document is addressed. A clean,

uncluttered cover appeals most. Churchill, referring to his own youth, described reactions to his reports by his prime minister: "A carefully-marshalled argument, cleanly printed ... often won his approval and thereafter commanded his decisive support."[2]

The minimum essential wording, the quality and color of the paper, and the overall design need periodic updating to provide ready access. Additionally, the binding process should enable a reader to lay the document flat, once opened. "Spines" that encroach on the margins or that require gymnastics to keep open or that eat up filing space cause irritation, extending to the content.

TRANSMITTAL

In a formal report, the opportunity to sound human, even personal, occurs chiefly in one spot. That spot is the transmittal letter or memo. It is this quick communication which says that the work is done and the results are ready in finished form. This part of the "package" may carry a reminder as to how the report originated, that is, the source of the request or authorization. It is signed by the human hand, although the name is rarely that of the actual author or authors. In managment consulting work, there is leeway about personal signatures. In public accounting firms the name signed is often that of the firm itself, and government agencies do the same. The exact handwriting may, by time-honored custom, be that of the senior partner or official.

The personalized aspect may extend to more than mere penman-ship, however. The transmittal is directed by name to the primary official among those on the receiving end, with other distribution sometimes noted. If the addressee is outside the auditor's professional "family" (if the auditor is not "internal," that is), the letter form is prepared with the heading, inside address, salutation, and compli-mentary close. If the recipient is inside (a management executive within the same organization or a grantee, for instance), the transmit-tal may be a memo, carrying the usual "To," "From," and "Subject" lines.

The first person singular ("I," "me," "my," and "mine") and the second person ("you," "your," and "yours") can keep the transmittal's tone conversational and personal. The first person plural ("we," "us," "our," and "ours") is used more frequently than the singular to represent the collective or corporate responsibility.

Acknowledgment of any courtesies extended during the course of the work can add a further human touch. Because the ensuing pages have to be impersonal, a contrasting preliminary tone offsets the sense of organizational facelessness.

Just as acknowledgment and thanks are due for facilitating the work, the opposite may at times be pertinent. It is possible that difficulties were encountered: Certain items of information may have been unobtainable; records may have been inaccessible, time may have proved insufficient for complete coverage; or changes in process may have precluded definitive conclusions. Such limitations, if pointed out initially, protect the writer.

As another possibility, the report's necessary objectivity is sometimes given a slightly subjective twist in the preceding letter or memo. An auditor may call attention to particular findings. To do so will, of course, slant the reader in a certain direction and for that very reason may not be desirable.

In one unusual indication of a deficiency in documentation, the particular need for a transmittal was specifically noted in the body of the report.

We could not determine the dates on which the reports were transmitted because the XYZ Manual does not require a letter of transmittal.

Quite apart from its traditional content there is an increasing trend to use the letter or memo as a summary of the report itself. When this is done, no separate digest is required, thereby simplifying the setup.

Brevity is the best policy in this personalized phase, the one-page limit being helpful. As little time as possible should elapse before the reader gets to the real beginning. If the whole document is to be double-spaced (to make the reading easier over the "long haul"), single spacing in the "short haul" of the transmittal will unify it and permit typographical differentiation of the various layers of format.

As to exactly where this personalized approach appears, reports differ. In unusual circumstances it is clipped on top of the cover; the primary recipient may then remove it if deemed unsuitable for all readers. At times, it is merely slipped under the cover, which also allows it to be removed. Customarily, the transmittal is bound in as an integral part of the whole presentation, recalling the pertinent circumstances surrounding the audit.

TITLE PAGE

After the cover and transmittal comes the title page. This page conveys more than the title: It repeats the title on the cover along with the source, but more details may be added, such as full identification of the addresses and their capacities. The title page puts together neatly the "situational" relationship of sender to receiver (the "who" and the "whom"), the subject and purpose (the "what" and the "why"), and the location and dating of the work (the "where" and the "when"). Usually the content and spacing of a title page follow a standard pattern, leaving few problems for the writer to decide.

TABLE OF CONTENTS

One of the earmarks of the formal report is the use of a table of contents, sometimes headed by the word "Contents." Informal reports (letters, letter reports, and memos) do not utilize this device. But when coverage and audience become complex, the readers need a road map to find their way through what lies ahead. If the whole table of contents can be confined to one page, the overview appears at one glance. It provides the first indication of the relationship of the parts to the whole. A complete table of contents, carrying the subheadings with any appended matter and graphics (exhibits), may take more than one page.

The skeleton type of a table of contents, with major or first-level headings only, looks like this:

CONTENTS

Part	Page
I. Introduction	1
II. Findings and Recommendations	5
III. General Information	27

From such minimal information, the reader does not know the nature of the findings or even how many there are. Yet there is a temptation to use such a "transferable" pattern, changing only the page numbers each time.

More informative is the detailed road map, showing what Churchill, in describing his method of organizing, called the "stations": "I write a book the way they built the Canadian Pacific Railway. First I lay the track from coast to coast, and after that I put in all the stations."[3]

The kind of thing Churchill had in mind as far as the table of contents is concerned can be illustrated in this way:

CONTENTS

Synopsis		Page
Part I.	Introduction	1
	A. Audit Period	2
	B. Scope	2
	C. Previous Reviews	4
Part II.	Operations Control	11
	A. Personnel	11
	B. Assignments	14
	C. Supplies	16

From such a detailed table of contents the reader can assume that the auditor found five problems in all, three for the attention of those in charge of operations and two for the budget planners. The outlining symbols (such as Roman numerals, capital letters, Arabic numbers, and small letters) are sometimes shown and sometimes dropped as a matter of preferred or prescribed practice, and the identifying symbols follow various systems. Accountants are familiar with this pattern:

1.

   1.1.

   1.2.

2.

   2.1.

      2.1.1.

      2.1.2.

   2.2.

      2.2.1.

      2.2.2.

Readers will expect the same wording and the same symbols to be repeated in the body.

Part IV in the model is intended for the "outsider" who needs data but is unfamiliar with the setting. "Inside" readers can turn selectively to the exact finding (say, page 24) that may be of particular applicability. If the initial recipient does not have to study each full finding, it is easy to pass the document along to those on the staff who will have the task of taking action. The top-level recipient may or may not feel obliged to read the whole report.

The wording in the headings must be parallel in structure. Headings are usually most easily expressed as the names of things, like the nouns and noun phrases in the model. Parallelism is expected at the same levels, though each level can be constructed differently. Headings may be carried down to no more than the first level (illustrated in the skeleton table) or to more (as in the second illustration).

Whether headings extend to the first, second, third, or fourth subdivision, at the same level they should be mutually exclusive, like these two:

A. Appropriations

B. Expenditures

They should not overlap, like these:

A. Finances

B. Appropriations

When subheadings are used, logic requires that there be a minimum of two. It is not possible to divide an apple and come up with only one piece. "Attachment A" presupposes at least an "Attachment B."

SYNOPSIS

With the preliminary pages out of the way, the formal report itself may commence with a synopsis to represent the unity and emphasis arising from all that is being reported. This part of the document may be entitled "Summary," "Digest," "Highlights of the Results," "Executive Brief," or something similar to Synopsis. Whatever is covered here conditions the reader to the total content that is to follow.

Sometimes this opening summary is all that will be read. The high-level recipient may not require the supporting details, particularly when the evidence has been discussed personally in preceding meetings or at the closing conference. Within each individual finding, the value of an initial summation is often achieved in the first paragraph. The condition, cause, criteria, effect, and even cure can all be given in capsule form.

For the main synopsis, however, this bird's-eye view of the entire content should include a sentence or two, or sometimes a short paragraph, about each special finding. The individual subunities, extracted from the report proper, appear in the order in which they come later, though the exact wording should not be duplicated. In anticipation of the following development, the proportioning of space should be comparable in order to reflect the final balance or emphasis.

Such a summary is most helpful at the outset of the whole report, especially when it can appear on a single page. Standing close under the front cover, it gives instant solidity. Because of the necessity for extreme selectivity in content and extreme economy in wording, it is hard to prepare. Short sentences permit speedy intake, and short paragraphs convey a feeling of rapid progression. The shorter the sentences and paragraphs, the more they need interconnecting by obvious transitions. Wherever there are separations, bridges are essential.

If such a unified digest is offered at the beginning, the writer will probably have also revealed the overall opinion. That being the case, directness of sequence is a foregone conclusion. No longer can the basic criticism or criticisms be withheld; no longer is it possible to play for time in order to explain "cause" (that is, reasons) before a reader knows the "effect." There may be instances where it is not wise to proceed so fast; then the indirect method is the alternative. The fact remains that the very sight of a digest implicitly promises the reader at the start that there will be no surprises later.

Recommendations are often but not always regarded as integral to the synopsis. If they are not included, the reader cannot be said to know the final thrust of the analysis; if included, they must be consolidated. The auditor has to ask the acid question: "If my recipient sees nothing but the summary, am I content to stand on that?" When the answer is "yes," there is reason to take pride in the authorship.

RESPONSE

Concurrence or nonconcurrence from the officials under review is ordinarily known before the final report gets between covers. The operational auditor will know from a face-to-face conference the reception accorded to the findings.

For a government report, the first response to the findings is usually by word of mouth. The oral medium, discussion, occurs throughout the course of working on each finding, not just at the formal exit or close-out conference. If rebuttal brings to light unsupported or unsupportable conclusions in a draft statement, the auditor then has the chance to make adjustments. Assuming that a finding stands without retraction or revision, the recipient's written response, whether negative or positive, may be incorporated to a greater or lesser extent in the published version: To quote:

> At an exit conference, the Director agreed to evaluate and, as appropriate, realign the work load. We believe this action, if properly implemented, will satisfy the intent of our recommendation.

The position and treatment of the response have undergone considerable rethinking. In the early days of operational audits, it seldom appeared at all. The report was regarded as the finalized utterance of the auditor in which there was no necessity for "listening" to the other party. Then, the respondents began to be heard more loudly, and writers themselves recognized the wisdom of including such reactions, albeit in abbreviated form, sometimes between parenthesis, or in fine print.

Now, the response is given more space. Auditors show no qualms about including a concurrence, finding by finding:

> The Director agreed to the recommendation for reclassification of personnel and is taking immediate action.

Gradually, a strategic value has been achieved in the process of representing more fully the responding views, whether pro or con the findings or the recommendations.

Written replies may be paraphrased so that the respondents are given their "day in court." Many responses are now accorded equal typographical treatment (not appearing in italics, parentheses, or reduced print):

> Our findings and recommendations were discussed with the Associate Director for Administration and his staff on January 21, 19__. Generally, they agreed with our conclusions and stated that, with respect to our recommendations, their reply to our report would show the corrective actions already taken or to be initiated.

Some reports go to the extent of quoting word for word the recipient's remarks under a suitable heading like "Reply," "Comments," "Action Taken," or "Auditee's Response." Whether such reaction is placed at the end of each condition or appears only at the end of the entire document is a matter which is influenced by the length of the necessary paraphrase or quotation:

Reply

> Management concurred with all ten recommendations, stating that pursuant measures would be taken at once:

—A system will be developed to require supervisory personnel to ensure maintenance services.

—A maximum of 5 days will be allowed for preparation of each job order.

[Only two of the ten measures are included here.]

If the respondent's own words are being given, it is essential either to indent or to use double quotation marks at the beginning of each quoted paragraph and at the end of the last one. In one instance, a memo was appended in its entirety:

SUBJECT: *Comments on Report of Policies and Practices Relating to Use of Administratively Uncontrollable Overtime*

We are in agreement that the Department should develop uniform policies and procedures governing administratively uncontrollable overtime, but we believe the development should be held in abeyance and completed in conjunction with the study on the average number of hours for work periods of employees involved in security activities as is required by Section 6(c)(3) of P.L. 93-259 entitled Fair Labor Standards Amendments of 1974.

It is recommended that the formula used to compute the average number of hours worked in a week be adopted department-wide. It more fairly compensates the employee for work performed.

The Administrative Manual was changed after discussion with the auditors. This is not accurate. The change was made as the result of claims made by employees for payments covering periods immediately following their entrance on duty.

When agreement is not achieved or only partially achieved and is so recorded, it still remains tactically wise for the auditors themselves to have the last word. After all, the reports are the auditors' reports. So, in the case of opposition to a finding or to an entire document, the final comment may be something like this:

Management's Reaction

Management agreed in part with the facts presented but did not agree with the recommendations. (For the full response, see Appendix.)

Auditor's Reaction

Management's views were considered prior to submission of this report. The circular or procedures (XYZ, Sec. II, Pars. a through k) as cited in the findings establishes the factual necessity for adequate stockage of parts. The provisions are also clear, in the case of shortages, as to where and how replenishments are to be obtained. Our recommendations are based on these provisions.

The closing position belongs not to the addressee but to the author.

GRAPHICS

Communication on paper need not be limited to words. Pictures (charts, tables, maps, exhibits, photographs, drawings) tell the story, too. The graphic aspect of a page begins with the effective use of margining, double and single spacing, blocking, enumerating, indenting, placing of headings, underlining, and capitalizing. From there the reader may be helped to move forward to such visual aids as colored dividers, tabs, or other guideposts.

Reports warranting very elaborate media contain between their covers overlays, transparencies, cutouts, or foldouts, all of which are used as attention-getting features in other publications but are not so well known in consultative reporting.

Whatever nonlinear medium is employed needs careful integration with the linear. An explanatory caption, sentence, or paragraph is needed to accompany an exhibit. Seldom is it necessary to use the overworked expression "the following" or "as follows." Readers can see that something graphic does indeed come next, but mechanical wording, such as "The chart illustrates the results of our review as follows," does not give them credit for noting the obvious. The purely mechanical, noninformative lead-in tells only what can be seen with one's own eyes: that a chart follows (the reader already knows that there has been a review from which results are to be expected). What the reader does not know but could benefit by hearing in advance is more substantive guidance such as:

> Between the two departments we reviewed, petty cash was unevenly expended:

By the same token, after looking at a graphic illustration, the reader needs similar reinforcement (again, in noninsulting terms) as to the point of what has been demonstrated or exhibited. The lead-out sentence or paragraph is a helping hand. Because of the popularity of pictures, reports are often reviewed, once they have been read, merely by studying the exhibits. Each graphic will speak for itself provided it is given its own caption or title.

The habit of lumping all graphics together in an appendix is changing. The reasons for this habit have been understandable. It is easier for the writer than fitting them into the body of the document and it eases the typing and duplicating processes. More validly, the withholding of detailed exhibits until the end prevents readers who do not need the detail from being interrupted. As still another consideration, a graphic that is referred to more than once in the body of a report cannot be repeated each time, in which case it may be placed in

an appendix, with appropriate cross references appearing in the body
of the report:

(For detailed distribution, see chart, Appendix, p. 32.)

The page reference adds convenience, while the parentheses reduce
the distraction.

The alternative position for the illustrative materials is within the
text itself right at the various points of impact. If a graphic is of true
significance, why not place it where the reader can refer to it without
being forced to look ahead and then back again to the textual
comment? Incorporation of a schematic less than one page in length
offers no problem. Likewise, if it consists of a whole page, the lead-in
sentence can be the last on the preceding page, and the lead-out
sentence can be the first on the succeeding page. Sometimes, the
easiest way to achieve correlation is to place the linear and the graphic
on facing pages so that both come into view simultaneously.

When graphics are mentioned more than once or when they
cannot be placed at the exact point at which they are mentioned,
figure numbers may be used in the captions with parenthetical figure
references in the text.

Strategic combination of well-placed graphics with the basic text
gives the captive reader welcome variation and convincing reinforcement of essential conditions. The reader starts by looking as well as
reading. A map (Figure 1), as one illustration, captures attention.

This is the age of graphic or pictorial input. Television, pictorial
signs, and photographs in newspapers and magazines have conditioned readers to glance as well as read and to expect more than mere
print on a page. Computer graphics can be prepared in full color and
seem to enlist more credibility than those done the old way. In
modern reports, the purpose is to show as well as tell, thereby
providing a change of pace and a reinforcement of the message. The
graphic medium must, however, serve the message, and not vice versa.
Auditors may steer away from such means, thinking it not within their
tradition, or they may hold back, feeling unable to be artists as well as
authors. But the balance sheet or financial statement, not to mention
the basic T-account, is itself a visual aid.

In regard to the tradition of audit reporting, there is a new and
growing trend toward being more boldly illustrative. Tradition has to
inch forward with the times if it is to be worth preserving. As for
hesitancy about going graphic, few who actually conceive and plan the
exhibits used in business reports are professional designers any more
than they are professional writers. The first prerequisite for adding the
look-and-see dimension is to recognize a point that can be neatly

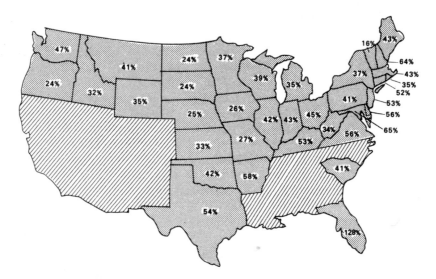

FIGURE 1   Growth in funding, 196* to 197*, for selected states.

shown in more than words. That is not hard once the imagination is given rein. For instance, the difference by age groups in the number of hours required to perform a fixed task like loading a truck lends itself to a line chart (Figure 2). The vertical legend of the graph represents the percentage of work hours, and the horizontal shows the age levels surveyed. For a variation, the line graph itself could be superimposed on a background photo of the activity being performed.

A pie chart (Figure 3), which takes only a compass and a ruler to execute, is the easiest of all. It may segment income expenditures, population growth, sources, or any whole divided by individual slices.

The bar chart (Figure 4) is another simple device with columns varying in height according to substances, areas, costs, or whatever

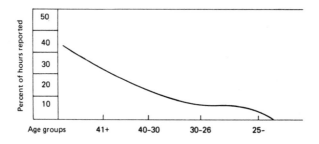

FIGURE 2   Hours required to load trucks.

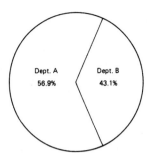

FIGURE 3 Petty cash expenditures by two departments.

needs comparing. Each bar may be divided crossways or sideways if subsets of the matters portrayed are complicated.

Very popular now is the flowchart. Data processors have made a science of it, but a simple flowchart requires no more than an instinct for logical progression along a "critical path." Charting a pathway from the beginning to the end of a series of interrelated steps means starting in an unmistakable spot, either top center or left; moving progressively by arrows or other obvious indicators in an unblocked direction; avoiding sidetracks; and ending at the planned destination. One such chart, slightly modified, is shown in Figure 5. Readers need to be allowed the sense of making it on their own without being stopped in their tracks or losing their way. Flowcharts suffer when the steady movement diverges or dead-ends.

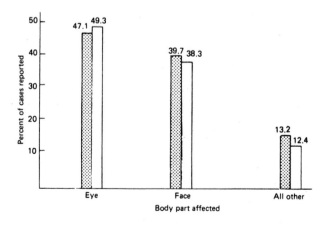

FIGURE 4 Distribution of injuries by body part for fiscal years 1982 and 1983. Key: shaded areas = FY 1982; white areas = FY 1983.

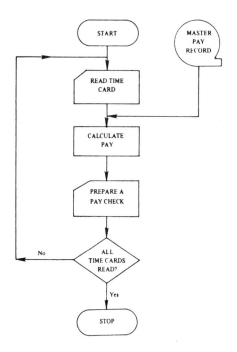

HOW TO PREPARE PAY CHECKS

FIGURE 5 A time card containing the number of hours worked and a master pay record containing information on rate of pay for an individual are read, the salary is calculated, and an appropriate paycheck is prepared for disbursement. (*General Accounting Office.*)

Pictograms (or pictographs), which use symbols to represent units such as people, buildings, or pieces of equipment, are one more of the many means by which a point can be illustrated with more than words. Floor plans, roadways, and diagrams are other devices that may be included, as well as an original concept for something not used before.

Most recently, photographs have been introduced into reports as incontrovertible evidence of equipment stored without protection, cash registers positioned below the counters, unsanitary housing, and stream pollution, for example. Such matters, if seen, need little verbal proof. Reproduction processes are developing so rapidly that the cost of the required number of copies may no longer be a deterrent, although color reproductions may be more expensive.

The difference between black-and-white and color photographic evidence was demonstrated by one specific investigative experience.

First a black-and-white print was developed of a picture taken at the scene of an automobile accident; it showed a substance that had spilled onto the sidewalk. The preliminary conclusion was that the substance was oil from the vehicle involved. Further investigation, including a photograph of the scene developed in color, showed that the stain was not black like oil, but red. Actually, it proved to be blood from one of the passengers, whose claim of injuries had been disputed.

APPENDIX

In keeping with the trend of simplified format, a hard decision has to be made as to whether appended "extras" are necessary after the body of the report. Such material consists of documents, explanatory detail, and sometimes exhibits. The one essential factor in defining an appended item is that it must be expendable; that is, whatever is appended may be skipped.

Information deemed to be nonessential for all, but helpful to some, may be included after the report proper has been ended. An appendix is used only for such items as readers may, if they wish, ignore. Just like the human body, a report may be at least as well off (if not better off) without the unnecessary matter. The writer who does decide to include this final attached portion may have several justifiable purposes in mind.

Typical operational audit appendixes consist of inventory records, charts of accounts or financial statements, itemized listings, sample records, and responses from auditees. For the specialist, such details may be of assistance. For the individual charged with implementing a recommendation, these extra specifications may prove instrumental.

The mere existence of appended evidence, scanned or unscanned, has an impact upon some skeptical readers. Even without reading, they see at the end what appears as further verification.

Increasingly, the appendix is becoming the repository of detailed information on the entity that has been studied. The primary recipients, normally those in charge of managing this entity, do not need to be told its size, purpose, location, or history. When the report's distribution list contains others with legitimate interests but less familiarity, explanatory facts can conveniently be screened out and held for the attachment, appendix, or annex.

Of course, the author may decide to face up to the hard decision of essentiality and save the extra time for preparing, writing, typing, and reading. Is the material needed, or is it not? If the decision is "yes," the material may be put where it fits into the report body. If it is "no," the material may be retained only in the workpapers. The temptation is to play the situation safe, to say "maybe yes, maybe no," and fall back upon the use of a catchall at the end. Warranted as such a device often is, streamlining of contemporary format is an argument for the gradual diminution of appended pages.

FINAL IMPRESSION

After looking separately at all these bits and pieces of a report's appearance, the writer must take into consideration the overall impression they make in conjunction with one another. If there is too much overlapping, redundancy becomes quickly apparent. Content is inevitably repeated in different guises. It is also apparent that the same content, presented in the consecutive phases of the format, acquires fresh emphasis. From the beginning to the end of a report, from cover to appendix, the process is one of accretion. The cover introduces; the transmittal personalizes; the title page sets the stage; the table of contents outlines; the synopsis summarizes and unites; the graphic material illustrates; the recipient's response contributes dialogue; and an appendix supplements.

Rather than seeming repetitive, full format should reinforce the major point or points at different stages. Individual writers seldom have control over how a report is to be designed. Matters such as the direct versus the indirect sequence may be fixed by an organization's manual, as well as the very appearance itself. How a report is put together, being one of the control factors in its success, is designed in advance for uniformity. The appearance of a document serves as either an inducement or a deterrent to the reader.

Because of this need for professionalized packaging, layout is usually planned and prescribed from the top down for all writers in a given group. The theory is that they should portray a consistent image. Although the designing of format may not be within the individual's power, the writer who wants to be creative may adjust and adapt the standardized pattern to fit particular circumstances. In the last analysis, each writer determines how words are to be put together. Similarly, each writer should determine how to mold ready-made format most fittingly for each message.

NOTES

[1] When one of the old-line federal departments experimented by replacing its long-familiar logotype with a contemporary design, public reaction persuaded the department to go back to its traditional, easily recognized symbol.

[2] Randolph S. Churchill, *Winston S. Churchill*, vol. 2: *Young Statesman: 1901–1914*, Houghton Mifflin Company, Boston, 1967, p. 517.

[3] Quoted in *The Ann Arbor News*, Jan. 28, 1965.

10 Strengthening content

The prime concern of those who are reporting to management is the subject matter itself. The truth is that the message is inseparable from the medium (that is, from style and organization). Whether the report-writers are public accountants, governmental auditors, internal reviewers, management consultants, investigators, or analysts, the meat of their reports is what counts most to them and to their receivers. Will the message be convincing? Will the findings gain concurrence? Will management take a constructive course of action?

EXPANSION OF COVERAGE

Since the early seventies, the extent of what has to be reported has taken on new dimensions. For one reason, Certified Public Accountants (CPAs) heretofore engaged to render opinions on financial matters now find themselves entering into working relationships with governmental auditors whose mission is to advise management on overall performance. A second reason is that management is looking for analysis not only of its probity but of its productivity as well. As analysts have sought to achieve such goals, the definition of scope, always crucial, has acquired further criticality.

Once scope is defined, the analyst's task is to formulate whatever is in need of change and, often, to propose the method for accomplishing the change. Some conditions identified call for extensive support.

Other matters like financial or legal discrepancies may speak for themselves.

Whatever the breadth and depth of a report, certain weaknesses in logical and psychological acceptability of the content are recurrent. Likewise apparent are certain practices that heighten credibility. Advisory reports will not meet the legitimate expectations of readers unless the writers make their subjects both clear and credible.

A deep-seated sense of responsibility was manifested by professional accountants in their reaction to the publication in 1977 by a United States Senate subcommittee of the "Metcalf report," *Improving the Accountability of Publicly Owned Corporations and Their Auditors.* When charged with a lack of independence, leaders in the profession were quick to counter the implications, emphasizing the American Institute of Certified Public Accountants' (AICPA) achievement of "the highest quality of financial reporting and disclosure of any country in the world" and stressing the profession's "commitment to the public interest."[1]

The terms "auditor" and "audit" differ among those using them. Although a difference exists between a purely financial audit and a managerial or program analysis, the separation is not hard and fast.[2] Some in business would reserve the word "audit" (1) for the public accounting firm's examination of financial statements and (2) for the internal reviewers' appraisal of their own organization. In spite of these attempts, usage has already stretched the meaning. A quality-assurance manager (not an auditor) reported that: "An audit was taken from May 10, 1977, to June 30, 1977, on the total number of packages rejected by the packaging machine." In government generally and in accounting firms increasingly, it is agreed that the definition of "auditing" has been expanded to include determination of compliance with applicable laws and regulations, detection of fraud, efficiency and economy of operations, and effectiveness of program results. Underlying reports entitled "audits" is the intent of evaluating, of drawing conclusions, and often of advising. Neither the inclusiveness nor the exclusiveness of subject matter is fixed for all time.

Disclosure

One thing is safe to say. The trend is toward more rather than less disclosure, as regards weaknesses and strengths alike: "The accounting profession must now reassess itself. Lagging, it has continued to offer simplistic, uni-dimensional, single-valued descriptions of an economic reality that has become complex, multidimensional and multivalued."[3]

Another point seems safe to emphasize. Finances are not locked into watertight compartments apart from operations. Dollar amounts talk and talk loudly as to the quality of performance. As one official statement summed it up: "A good audit begins with a good set of books."[4] Money and mission go hand in hand, but danger arises if ". . . a company's management of human resources, whether for good or ill, goes undetected in financial statements."[5] The individual who is a CPA possesses a hard core of specialized knowledge on which to test accountability.

At the same time, the best-qualified accountant finds it impossible to judge performance without learning about the management's activities as a whole. Experts in many fields are being called in to join audit staffs:

> If any organization possesses personnel, or hires outside consultants, with acceptable skills in such areas as accounting, statistics, law, engineering, and actuarial science, each individual member need not possess all these skills.[6]

The advent of the computer has added, literally, tons of data, compiled with electronic speed, upon which to draw. Relevant as this evidence is, writers do not always know how to cope with the volume of printouts. Such information has actually been misleading, as in the case of the Equity Funding scandal, where "External auditing of this company failed to detect any problems for three years. . . ." Reporting of financial processes has proved susceptible to abuse via the computer. Numerous "computer crimes" have not been discovered through normal security precautions or accounting controls.[7]

The elements in what the AICPA describes as expanded-scope audits have been set forth by that body for CPAs to use in responding to government requests for help.[8] The challenges to the practitioners in governmental work are immense: "These . . . opportunities for the CPA, his firm, and his profession . . . are certainly as great as, if not greater than, those in the private sector."[9]

One instrument of growing assistance among co-workers in circumscribing the number of areas to be examined is the survey. Surveys are preliminary documents that describe an organization, activity, or program. On the basis of such an initial approach, an audit manager determines whether there are probable findings.

Scope

The precise scope of a report is delineated in the introduction. In financial reports, scope has been highly standardized. The period and the location are identified, in addition to the regular statement referring to "such tests . . . and other auditing procedures as we considered necessary. . . ." In expanded reporting, a statement of the functions to be examined provides self-insurance for the writers and advance warning for the readers as to what is going to be ruled in and what is going to be ruled out, as shown in two illustrations:

> ... management of the Equipment Maintenance Section (Motor Pool) was reviewed. . . . A detailed examination of all transactions was not made. Tests of records and procedures were made to the extent necessary.
>
> ... financial records, unit checkbooks, supply registers and receipts were reconciled on a selective basis. . . .

Practical limitations

A realistic consideration in limiting scope is how much effort can be afforded to full-scale operational analysis. How much content can be soundly developed within deadlines and dollar ceilings? How many leads can be followed by investigators? "Hotlines," announced by certain government agencies as being open to the public for calling in suspected wrongdoing, have produced a quantity of information, some verifiable and some not. "Hotline" leads must be followed. The decision as to whether to sustain certain conditions is based upon their materiality: "Is it practical to audit a $2 billion company for $50,000 items? This question was raised in *The Wall Street Journal.*[10] The cost of looking into all the nooks and crannies has at times seemed prohibitive.

Another reason for circumscribing an analysis is to offset the view voiced by some in responsible quarters that auditors may not be truly independent of their clients in managerial matters: "If the accountant approaches the audit, with a predisposition—whether conscious or otherwise—to validate management's work rather than to subject it to careful scrutiny, then the ultimate result will be diminution of public confidence in the profession and in business generally. . . ."[11]

Yet coverage that is regarded as less than complete is also attacked. Officials have demanded to know where the auditors were when bodies receiving governmental subsidy, like the Pennsylvania Central, suffered bankruptcy or other disaster. The Securities and Exchange Commission (SEC) stated that the Penn Central's financial reports were not an adequate indication because ". . . the economic substance was not properly reflected therein and because there was insufficient attention given to the overall conditions of the company and its operations."[12]

Not only do public officials protest, but clients also feel aggrieved when losses allegedly arise from auditors' oversights or negligence. It was estimated, in the mid-1970s, that 300 suits were outstanding against fewer than a dozen large accounting firms.[13]

Different attitudes

For the CPA firm engaged to perform an external audit for a client, extent of disclosure is a problem. It is not of such concern for the internal auditor because the results are intended for the eyes of the organization's own management. For governmental auditors, disclosure is usually a foregone conclusion, so reports are prepared with that in mind.

One partner in a "Big Eight" firm attributes the restrictiveness of coverage to the profession's being hidebound by his own history: "Our measurement process is so restricted, given the flow of events in today's economic environment, that we are all caught up in a set of rules that gives us reverse tunnel vision—an inability to look around us or ahead of us, an unwillingness to attempt to predict future events."[14] He advocates the "what if" attitude, whereby a business may foresee the outcome of new ventures. Such an attitude, if part of the consulting work of an audit firm, whether this work is regarded as an "audit," "analysis," or "study," would be protective, even preventive, as regards mistakes. Forward orientation as well as the historical approach has been conspicuous in the work of particular national and state agencies.

People working for CPA firms and for governmental bodies find their paths crossing more and more. One may be auditing the other. One may be assisting the other to perform one part of an undertaking. They may work jointly on the same assignment. Governmental auditors are expected to ferret out causes and effects, financial and programmatic, in their reports. More explicit instructions have therefore become essential for joint endeavors.

Standards

In the face of differing traditions, both public and private sectors have made available written guidelines for the components of their reports. The standards are applicable to a broader scope than formerly, as one AICPA source indicates:

> It appears unlikely that criteria will be documented that can be applied in all situations because of the diversity of government operations and program goals. This makes it essential that the practitioner use professional judgment as to the appropriateness of the criteria used in a specific engagement. Sources for such criteria include legislative language; agency standards, policies and procedures; responsible agency management personnel; contractual terms; previous experience with similar activities; and authoritative publications on the subject.[15]

As objectivity rests upon criteria, agreement upon the basis of measurement is a necessity. The point is to stand on tangible principles. CPAs acting through the AICPA and the Financial Accounting Standards Board (FASB) have issued numerous aids, among them *Guidelines for CPA Participation in Government Audit Engagements to Evaluate Economy, Efficiency and Program Results*.

The federal government, acting through the General Accounting Office (GAO), has also issued mandatory guides, chief of which is *Standards for Audit of Governmental Organizations, Programs, Activities, and Functions*. Just as CPA firms quote pertinent AICPA and FASB criteria in their reports (as codified in *Statements of Auditing Standards*), governmental auditors at the different levels cite the GAO's publication:

> Directorate of Audit and Investigation performed an examination of transactions, accounts and reports, and an evaluation of compliance with applicable laws and regulations, in conformity with the "Standards for Audit of Governmental Organizations, Programs, Activities &. Functions" issued by the U.S. General Accounting Office....[16]

The AICPA and GAO each acknowledge the other's standards for the purposes of co-working. Writers reporting joint effort on unprecedented areas now have compatible criteria to which all taking part can refer.

RANGE OF SUBJECTS

The appeal as well as the risk in the reporting task lies in the diversity of managerial problems. The reporting obligation, which was once confined to the familiar scope of fiscal affairs, must now take into account a host of less familiar concerns. In the amplification of accountability, co-workers of comparable diversity may be involved: an auditor working with a lawyer, an accountant working with an investigator, an engineer working with an environmentalist, and a data processor working with almost everyone.

Specific topics

A random listing of individual subjects taken from reports of recent audits by CPAs and others in both government and industry shows the variety:

Park concessions

Aircraft maintenance

Solid waste disposal

Ballet troupes

Patient care

Trucking of supplies

River pollution

Community health services

Hair dyes

Sale of a floating bridge

Drug control

Flood containment

Electronic devices

Meat plants

Transshipment of grain

Rental and purchase of equipment

Length of employees' lunch hour

Hearing conservation

Discounts to subcontractors

Welfare checks

Nature of investments (including arbitrage)

Nursing homes

Coin-operated machines.

This list is merely the tip of the iceberg; the whole concept of "human resource accounting" lies under the waterline. Although the topics named merely suggest all audited areas, it is apparent that report-writers, moving from one of the topics to the next, cannot be specialists in all fields, nor should they be. In fact, independence is better assured when the nonspecialist is doing the critical reporting. Management is engrossed with its own efforts to meet public and private needs in money matters, in personnel, in productivity, and in program requirements.

The independent-minded analyst, possessed of a healthy curiosity, depends on asking questions and looking around. Such an "outsider" retains a perspective as to operational stability, regulatory compliance, and fiscal integrity, regardless of the field. In coping with the multiplicity of material, basic financial training provides the starting point, although it is not the stopping point, of a report. As one auditor explained: "When you're out on the job, you have to realize the connection between financial accounting, efficiency and economy and program effectiveness. If you're auditing equipment, consider not only if it's on hand but why is it on hand? For what reason was it purchased? How is it being used?"[17]

Professional skills

No matter what the nature of the exact subject at an exact site, auditors know how, when, and where to apply their own professional training in matters like:

Record keeping

Cash management

Data processing

Eligibility factors

Procurement

Regulatory requirements

Grants

Contracts

Vending

Internal controls

Security

Quality assurance

Supply

Testing (including sampling)

Personnel practices

Administrative procedures.

Acquaintance with computer science becomes an essential asset.

In the evaluation of automated (electronic) data processing systems, bypassing of built-in controls, lack of security in regard to access, and fraudulent manipulation of information must be detected. Management information systems are mounting in sophistication. Their reliability must be tested on the basis of stringent standards. Auditors are instructed to review not only the application but the design of data processing systems.[18] Many organizations have developed programs for application in evaluating performance. Recent though computer-based techniques may be, such techniques have already become a requisite for true professionalism.[19]

Common sense, though open to interpretation as to what is "common" and what is "sense," is the starting point of professionalism. Qualitative judgments are undeniably involved. One city auditor wrote, in the course of revealing municipal waste: "We found a fair amount of people running off with money."[20] It did not take more than common sense to recognize that something was wrong. In another instance, at a day-care center for children, it was observed that: "...

two sewer lines were located in the kindergarten room. One line had a loosely fitting wooden cap and was plugged with a baby doll."[21] Who will dispute the need for corrective action?

The public looks to auditors to track down and report succinctly the causes as well as the effects of mismanagement. In turn, the auditors have far-ranging fields over which to apply their own professional measures.

Corrective action

The attest function as conveyed in the unqualified opinion of a financial examination is not usually a component of management auditing. Using "opinion" in its particularized sense, an AICPA publication is explicit: "No auditor is expected to give an opinion of how efficient or economical an organization is or whether program results have been effectively achieved."[22] It is a fact that operational audit reports do not normally contain opinions in the standardized sense of financial reporting.[23]

Whereas the opinion statement is the earmark of financial reports, recommendations characterize operational reports. The short-form (financial) audit does not specify needed improvements. Such information is included in management letters. The recommendations which accompany governmental audits are not prescriptive in nature; they are advisory. For a negative condition, a "cure" is proposed. It is incumbent upon the advisory writer to propose to management personnel an altered course that would be conducive to realization of recognized goals. The report only proposes; it does not direct. The dividing line remains clear, and the independence of the adviser stays intact. In no way can the role of the manager be usurped. Only by preserving this division of labor do analysts retain their objectivity.

True, the seriousness of conditions as reported may demand quick action. Violation of criteria may be obvious. Cause may be beyond doubt, and the adverse effect irrefutable. The choice of remedial measures, however, remains with the recipient.

Detailed recommendations, if they are to be acceptable to those responsible for making changes, should be worded so as to make the action seem easy, frequently providing motivation for their adoption: potential dollar savings, perhaps, or a reduction in staff hours, or a decrease in delays:

Recommendation: Deadline surveillance should be recorded to afford the industrial specialist instant visibility of situations requiring immediate attention. Surveillance in accordance with specified deadlines will reenergize timely production.

Written presentation of recommendations does not appear to pose a problem. Most are stated positively, specifically, and convincingly. More difficulty lies in the way in which the original condition itself, not the corrective action, is formulated. Readers' receptivity is the test of the wording as well as of the content of the whole finding.

In some reports, a response is officially required, regardless of acceptance or rejection. Military reviews ordinarily end with citation of a regulation calling for response (concurrence or otherwise) within a fixed number of days. In New York State, a 1977 statute requires audited agencies to reply in writing to findings within 30 days so that the reply can be incorporated into the report as released.[24]

WHOLE IN RELATION TO PARTS

Granted that different types of reports require different proportions, depth of coverage is increasing. The pressure of public opinion as well as official regulations underlie the trend of the accounting profession toward the expansion of scope in auditing. Although the nature of coverage is increasing, in the extensive and intensive sense, the time for writing all the reports now being demanded is not increasing.

Uncertainty over what parts to include in a report slows up writers. Should a formal opinion be stated? Are recommendations appropriate? Standardized practices, though they have been and will continue to be subject to change, provide a source of reassurance.

The development of self-assurance regarding how much must be disclosed will speed up the process of reporting. Another source of self-confidence is the current clarification of standards between the once separate public and private sectors. There is now available an abundance of data from the computer's automatic processing, and from statistical sampling. Language remains the human instrument for turning information to account. In closing the communication gap, new successes as well as new stresses and strains await all writers in the working world.

NOTES

[1] *The New York Times*, Jan. 17, 1977. © 1977 by The New York Times Company. Reprinted by permission.

[2] See general comments of Ellsworth H. Morse, Jr., "Performance and Operational Auditing," *Journal of Accountancy*, vol. 131, no. 6, June 1971, pp. 41–46.

[3] Joshua Ronen, quoted in *The New York Times*, May 5, 1977. © 1977 by the New York Times Company. Reprinted by permission.

[4] United States Senate, Subcommittee on Reports, Accounting and Management of the Committee on Governmental Affairs, *Improving the Accountability of Publicly Owned Corporations and Their Auditors*, Government Printing Office, Washington, 1977, p. 13.

[5] Ronen, quoted in *The New York Times*, May 5, 1977. © 1977 by The New York Times Company. Reprinted by permission.

[6] United States General Accounting Office, *Standards for Audit of Governmental Organizations, Programs, Activities, and Functions*, 1981 Revision, Government Printing Office, Washington, p. 16.

[7] Donn B. Parker, Susan Nycom, and S. Stephen Oura, *Computer Abuse*, Stanford Research Institute, Menlo Park, Calif., 1973, p. 3.

[8] See, among other sources, American Institute of Certified Public Accountants, Management Advisory Services, *Guidelines for CPA Participation in Government Audit Engagements to Evaluate Economy, Efficiency and Program Results*, Guideline Series no. 6, New York, 1977.

[9] AICPA Committee on Governmental Accounting and Auditing, *Industry Audit Guide—Audits of State and Local Governmental Units*, New York, 1974, p. 5.

[10] *The Wall Street Journal*, June 12, 1975.

[11] United States Senate, Subcommittee on Reports, Accounting and Management of the Committee on Governmental Affairs, *Improving the Accountability . . . , p. 5.*

[12] Quoted in *The Philadelphia Inquirer*, July 8, 1975.

[13] *The New York Times*, Nov. 23, 1975.

[14] James T. Powers, quoted in *The New York Times*, June 2, 1974. © 1974 by the New York Times Company. Reprinted by permission.

[15] AICPA, Management Advisory Services, *Guidelines for CPA Participation . . . , p. 21.*

[16] From an unpublished report of the U.S. Department of Labor.

[17] An auditor quoted in *The New York Times*, Dec. 2, 1977. © 1977 by The New York Times Company. Reprinted by permission.

[18] United States General Accounting Office, *Additional GAO Audit Standards—Auditing Computer-Based Systems*, Government Printing Office, Washington, 1979, p. 4.

[19] See United States General Accounting Office, *Standards for Audit of Governmental Organizations, Programs, Activities, and Functions*, 1981 Revision, Government Printing Office, Washington, pp. 40–44. Appendix 1, pp. 57–62 on "Auditing Computer-Based Systems . . ." was added in the 1981 revision to the original 1972 *Standards . . .*, which did not cover the use of mechanical data processing.

[20] *The New York Times*, Dec. 17, 1970. © 1970 by The New York Times Company. Reprinted by permission.

[21] *The New York Times*, Dec. 15, 1974. © 1974 by The New York Times Company. Reprinted by permission.

[22] AICPA, Committee on Governmental Accounting and Auditing, *Industry Audit Guide*, p. 39.

[23] See also AICPA, Management Advisory Services, *Guidelines for CPA Participation . . .*, p. 10.

[24] *The New York Times*, Dec. 2, 1977.

11 Reinforcing credibility

The major point of expanded audit reporting consists of the statement of the adverse condition. This usually stands as the first sentence in each of a series of findings, followed immediately by the criteria, the cause, the effect, and sometimes the "cure" (that is, the gist of the recommendations that will be detailed subsequently). In strengthening the report of problems and in convincing readers of the need for recommended solutions, certain precautions must be observed, both logical and psychological in nature.

PROOF OF PROBLEMS

The writer must formulate each problem carefully and yet concisely if it is to be validly supported. The level of justification can then be determined in the interests of verifiability.

Formulation of condition

Before other factors, the deficiency itself must be pinned down. That alone suffices to introduce some findings:

Cash receipts: We observed certain weaknesses in handling cash receipts:

1. Checks were not stamped "For Deposit Only" when the mail was opened.

2. No list of cash receipts was made out at the initial opening of the mail.

3. Three employees handled the incoming checks before a listing was prepared. One of the three employees was the accounts receivable bookkeeper.

4. An adding machine tape was run by one of the three employees, but the total of this tape was not compared with the total bank deposit which was eventually made.

Until the criticism has been spelled out, the other attributes (elements considered essential in a finding) lack relevance. Only by the exercise of strict mental discipline can a short, candid sentence be framed that will afford the recipient a quick grasp. Codifying the negative factor demands disciplining the writer's thought process:

> Branch offices did not carry out procedures for monitoring land acquisitions.

This opening, setting forth an observed situation, is direct without sounding accusatory on the one hand or timid on the other.

Too much sidestepping is as detrimental as too much blame. Burying the weaknesses makes serious matters sound less serious. Real objectivity on the part of those reporting protects them from sounding like either a prosecutor or a Pollyanna. By means of straight thinking, the writer will make the critical condition self-evident. There is no more need for a string of "nots" than for repeated "sidesteps." When tempted to fall back upon such handy clichés as "improvement is needed," the writer has only to force the analytical process to the next phase: In what aspect is improvement needed? Are stricter controls essential? Is air quality below standard? Should accounts receivable be reduced?

The formulation of a problem, according to Einstein, often proves more essential than its solution, which, for him, became merely a matter of mathematics and experimental skill. Once the deficiency has been formulated in the light of established standards, on the basis of the observed effect, and in correlation with the cause, than the remedy may be obvious: "Developing specific findings is the heart of this [operational] audit."[1] Attempts to force through weak or vaguely worded findings merely to come up with a report will prove untenable. Productivity in reporting has to be measured by quality, not quantity.

Level of support

When the problem at stake has been forthrightly introduced, the next decision relates to the amount of support that will be needed to convince the recipients of its importance. Although an introduction containing the various attributes constitutes a capsule version of the whole finding, further explanation has to follow as background for any who might need it.

The more obvious the point is, the fewer the background details that are needed: "The importance of a problem should not be judged by the number of pages devoted to it."[2] Even the slightest cuts will save space and avoid affronts to the reader's intelligence:

> Review of 20 cost sharing reports disclosed that half (10) reflected differences.

The senior reviewer wrote in the margin:

> Why talk down to the reader? I'm insulted when I'm told that half of 20 is 10.

Deficiencies in money matters may require inclusion of only the pertinent financial statements, though the notes to these statements are growing in importance. Suspected fraud or abuse is sometimes reported briefly to the appropriate management official on the "flash" basis, often ending up in referral for criminal investigation and legal action.

A minimum of discussion is permitted in reports written for the military. Knowing that their management possesses the power of command, report-writers pare down their proof. There is no place for truisms (elaboration of the obvious). The first thing to cut would be statements like these:

> Determination of staff size is indispensable for effective management.

> The majority of errors is attributable to caseworkers and would be preventable with perfect casework.

Some reports drop all reference to inadequacies that are corrected as soon as they are pointed out. Other reports make mention of them in a sentence or two, noting that changes have already been effected. To curtail coverage in such a way is acknowledgedly a bargaining strategy to enlist acceptance of more important changes. Infrequently, report-writers develop manuals or procedures. Auditors who go too far in implementing their own advice are in danger of assuming managerial functions and jeopardizing their own independence when it comes to the eventual results.

Reports requiring in-depth support include those dealing with social resources in general. Their contents are more open to resistance. Such subject matter calls for greater support. A representative of a "Big Eight" firm, testifying before Congress, pointed out that: "... there is an unmistakable trend toward more detailed reporting...."[3] A climate of public distrust regarding big business and big government leads to point-by-point corroboration of facts revealed.

Convincing backup draws upon careful explanation of the methodology used in collecting data. One criticism requiring substantiation was this:

> Subsequent to submission of price data specifying average charges for the contract items to educational users, the contractor continued to charge more to this class of customer.

The method employed by the auditor to arrive at this point was then given:

> We ascertained the average rate actually charged to the educational customer. The specified prices were averaged and compared for each contract item from the effective date of the contract. Where the comparison showed an increase over the charges submitted with the contract proposal, we computed an average percentage. (See details of sales in Appendix.)

The conclusion drawn from this discussion of the reported excess in pricing led to a recommendation for refund of an exact dollar amount to educational customers.

Definitions are means of support that justify the space they take. They will be of growing assistance as new fields come under analysis. Specialized terminology carried over without explanation from source documents may be meaningless or ambiguous and thus open up danger zones. Definitions of common words that are used in an uncommon sense are also helpful.

One way to define, according to S. I. Hayakawa, is to give examples.[4] Concretely worded examples are easy to visualize. They are also verifiable, whereas the abstract statement being illustrated may be subject to question:

> A review of the receiving section for a 3-month period showed that only 53 percent of production was reported under the work measurement systems. For example, freight bills in December showed that 69,252 production units were processed through receiving sites, but only 35,231 units were reported.

In this excerpt, the first sentence is the generalized one with which a reader might take issue. The second sentence, containing the illustration, is not likely to be disputed; the bills themselves could be shown. To serve its purpose, an example must be judiciously selected so that it does not appear to be the one case that would lend credence to the writer's view. The choice must be made for representativeness and significance as well as for verifiability.

Balancing such favorable instances as can be found against the unfavorable may be worth the space:

> We tested sales data and determined that the majority of Contractor's monthly records for the Contracting Officer was accurate.

The trend in reporting on operations is definitely in the direction of constructiveness: "Since one of the main purposes of evaluation engagements is to assist management in improving operations, the practitioner should strive to emphasize the positive in reporting.... Too often omission of favorable comments completely distorts the perspective of the reader."[5]

Verifiability

Before forming judgments, auditors must observe factual circumstances. Their own inquiries, discussions, inspection of records, and notation of work flow are among their immediate sources. Inquisitiveness may be the best approach. Data drawn firsthand are descriptive in presentation, not analytical. The facts observed are verifiable only as of the time when noted. They are therefore best stated in the past tense:

> We noted that the employee's receipt for the purchases were not returned at the time of our audit.

The questions to be raised in the course of fact-gathering are often suggested in audit guides. Yet there is always the possibility that an entirely unanticipated problem will be uncovered. In this connection, the preliminary work of internal reviewers who have been on site and are intimately acquainted with day-to-day operations can help the external reviewers. Cooperative relations increase the information of both parties.

Quotations, like firsthand observations, are solid evidence. Especially useful in examining compliance are short quotations from statutes, administrative regulations, and manuals on management's policies and procedures. Excessive quoting, which makes readers impatient to the point of skipping, can be a temptation. Brief, well-placed excerpts are another matter:

> The standard practice guide states that:
>
> > Travel Expense Reports must be signed by the traveler and approved by an authorized signer on the amount to be charged.

All the details gathered, those which are relevant and some that may prove irrelevant, are recorded in the workpapers. Their accessibility to the supervisory members of a reporting team provides more support than has to be carried forward into the draft. From the workpapers, recurrent situations can be consolidated to establish patterns of performance.

Getting the right degree of backup depends upon the relative subjectivity of the criticisms and upon the relative sensitivity of the recipients. Glaring financial errors speak for themselves. Too many examples and quotations are as ineffective as too few. Estimating the appropriate amount of confirming data is a professional decision: "Deciding what to say is like passing through a cafeteria line and selecting a few items to make a balanced meal.... How we make our selection has a material bearing on the effectiveness of the report."[6] Once the items of content are selected, cohesiveness depends upon avoiding certain frequent pitfalls in reasoning.

CAUTION POINTS

Facts, if collected with thoroughness and arrayed without bias, make a strong case, but the logic underlying their presentation must be made indisputable. In bringing out cogent connections, authors should be on guard against a few traps in the analytical portions.

Loopholes

Loopholes are often left in the facts or in the logic that links them together. This happens because writers take it for granted that readers know or remember more than they do. Such a gap is easy to see:

> There are six other state schools and forty-four county homes which we did not review but whose procedures are carried out along the same lines as the eight facilities we did review.

If no review was made of the six schools and the forty-four homes, how can it be said that their procedures are carried out like those of the eight facilities that were reviewed?

Loopholes occur likewise in the steps of reasoning that have been taken:

> The custodians stated that they were unaware of the limitation on spending. As a result, they could not be reimbursed.

Because custodians were unaware of a limitation would not automatically prevent them from being reimbursed. Upon being asked to explain such lapses, writers usually have the answers on the tips of their tongues. Only on paper is there a blank.

Cause and effect

A particular kind of short circuit between fact and judgment comes from faulty combination of cause and effect: the *non sequitur* (literally translated from the Latin as "it does not follow"). *Non sequiturs,* defined in American dictionaries as inferences that do not follow from their premises, are strewn throughout functional reports, perhaps because authors, trained to think in terms of cause and effect, overwork the connection:

> Because a topic is more current, the readers will be more receptive.

The instinctive response is: "Not necessarily." Again:

> The branch was unaware of the extent of the asset shortages because differences in the physical inventory were unresolvable.

Just because inventory differences could not be resolved would not always lead to unawareness of shortages in assets. In a military audit, one *non sequitur* read:

> Since there were no family quarters on the post, the dining facility attracted the lower-grade enlisted men quartered there.

Many such illogical combinations could be corrected if the authors supplied in writing the thoughts that have stayed in their own heads.

Fact and inference

Drawing convincing conclusions out of data is the major task in drafting an evaluative document. From the writer's rational implications the reader is expected to draw the natural inferences. Neither the implications nor the inferences will produce the desired impact unless factuality is openly distinguished from inferential material. Ethically, the writer needs to signal the reader when moving from observed evidence into the arena of judgment. This clear separation between advocacy and the reporting of events "applies to communication in all the media," in the view of a major corporation's chief executive.[7] When readers are not notified of where they are being led, they are soon on guard against assertions like this:

> The Authority Commissioners admitted that (1) about $18,000 disappeared and (2) the shortage had not been reported. The Commissioners tried to cover up the shortage by using current cash receipts to make up for prior reports.

The first sentence represents fact; the second (containing the words "tried to cover up") seems to represent the writer's hypothesis but is not noted as such.

Normally, auditors use the words "in our opinion" or "we believe" to indicate that they are expressing a judgment or opinion. The weaker words "appear" and "apparently" are other signals authors use to show that they are moving from the known to the hypothetical. The heading "Recommendation" and the words "we recommend" also put readers on notice. Commingling of fact and inference, if discovered in one spot by readers, raises doubts about the trustworthiness of the whole logic.

Absolutes

Writers' credibility may also be shaken by a habit of universalizing, that is, of going beyond the general to the absolute:

> A record was never made of any of the transactions over past years.

The "accused" will feel like searching for the one single instance to the contrary, thus undermining all else. Exaggeration is suspected when terms such as "never," "none," "all," "every," "any," "always," and "each" appear. If the universe is carefully limited, the logic is not suspect. Universalizing may be accounted for by a writer's mistaken notion of emphasis. Sweeping declarations invite refutation:

> The new record-keeping method eliminated all possibility of error.

Caution is more convincing.

References to sampling

One special kind of loophole occurs in reporting on the use of sampling. For most fact-gatherers, knowledge of sampling has become a tool of their trade. How they explain their methodology is essential to the understanding of what the sample signifies. The General Accounting Office stipulates that if the task requires use of statistical sampling techniques, "... the staff or consultants to the staff must include persons with statistical sampling skills."[8]

When first introduced to audits some years ago, the methodology was often spelled out, including a decimal-pointed "confidence level," with more detail than many readers understood. The pendulum then swung to a minimum of explanation:

> We took a sample of 115 cases from the case file and determined that the securities were incorrectly handled in 60 cases.

The doubting reader is left to wonder: What percentage of the total does 115 cases represent? That is, how important a part of the total is the sample? How was the sample chosen? Statistically? Randomly? Or, as the handler of the securities may think, judgmentally, with a bias for incorrect cases? If the last was the basis of selection, the reader is entitled to know the nature of the judgmental selection. If statistical or random means were employed, the results have to be regarded as soundly derived, even though they may still be resisted:

Surveillance by Industrial Specialists

Problems were noted in surveillance practices in 118 of 196 randomly selected items. The 196 constituted 10 percent of all items produced. The problems noted included:

a. Inadequate inspection

b. Delayed plant visits

c. Preannounced schedule of surveillance.

Disclosure of the size of the universe from which the sample was taken and of the manner in which the sample was drawn seems to be the least that report-writers owe their readers and themselves. Giving the confidence level provides further credibility. If projections are then made from the sample, reference to the fact that a projection has been made should be clearly stated. In spite of occasional distrust of the best sampling techniques, those techniques need more specification in most reports.

Comparisons

Another weakness lies in the appearance of incomplete comparisons. A writer, fully versed in the subject matter, may state that:

The number of errors added up to more.

"More than what?" the reader has to ask if context does not contain the basis for the comparison. As a second illustration:

The other funds were used for supplies.

"Other than what?" will be asked if this has not been previously identified. The explanations remain locked in the report-writer's own mind. Lack of realization of the reader's inability or unwillingness to fill in the missing links is again the reason.

Credibility of content is strengthened when loopholes in facts or in logic are filled, when cause and effect are properly combined, when a signal is given before moving from fact to inference, when universalizing is held down to the believable, when sampling is sufficiently explained, and when the basis for a comparison is given.

END RESULTS

Simplifying language for practical intake requires more than rule books. It requires understanding of the needs and interests of the readers.

Simplification starts with writers' confidence in their facts and conclusions. They must then penetrate their own underlying intentions. Are they really willing to avoid the "safety" of ambiguities and obscurities? Are they really willing to cut their messages down to size instead of seeking to impress by length? Are they really willing to consider the needs and interests, but not the "wants," of their readers?

Accuracy of content cannot be communicated without the language skills that produce clarity. Even accurate, clear reports will not be read unless they are brief. Brevity, being relative to content, has to be measured not by bulk alone but by reading time and the value received therefrom.

Instrumental to rapid intake is directness. When writers decide, in advance, what the key point of a given report or of an individual finding is and present that first, the result is directness. Readers' demands for "getting to the point" will be fulfilled.

Being accurate, brief, clear, and direct are the theoretical goals almost universally named by practical communicators. Readers are in agreement with these objectives. To make the communication process two-way between adviser and manager, mental discipline must be rigorous. Do writers honestly intend to practice what they preach about their goals? Can readers accept the hard instead of the soft answers?

For all who respond affirmatively to these questions, gamesmanship in word play, in twisted sentences, or in devious paragraphs has no place. The avowed aims get only lip service when tricks are played. Yet candor is not enough; the candid statement must be made logically and psychologically acceptable to those on the receiving end. An "audit trail" must run through the writer's thought processes as through the factual delineations. Tone that is constructive will induce changes; tone that is destructive will meet with defensive tactics.

Operational auditors, by professional commitment, undertake three basic tasks in their reports: identification of negative factors, if any; suggestions, with feasible specifications of corrective actions; and details supporting these key points. Omission of any one of the three elements results in something other than a full-fledged report.

So rapidly has the operational audit evolved that those playing a part in its evolution have been pioneers without realizing it. Whereas standard format, like the management letter and the precast, short-form audit report, was enough to meet many needs in the past, changing scope and added criteria confront today's report-writers. There is a new kind of message being issued which calls for new skills.

The implications of auditing now represent an enlarged sphere. Content remains rooted in financial facts, but the purpose often is to measure performance against recognized objectives. When the performance does not measure up to standards, the reasons for the condition must be traced to their source. The effect, actual or potential, of the substandard condition may be shown in dollars and cents, in use of unnecessary work hours, in delays of essential actions, in lack of requisite procedures, or in total failure of a mission.

Once the analysis of the situation has been completed in the writer's own mind and factually recorded in notes and workpapers, expression of the analytical material in finished form is eased by following some sort of timetable:

1. Start drafting concurrently with fieldwork.

2. Aim to do the writing in "prime time" (decide whether morning, afternoon, or evening is best).

3. Prepare an initial outline from rough notes but keep the outline flexible.

4. Find a place in which to draft that suits individual preferences (perhaps an office with the door closed and no telephone calls or an open area with familiar sounds and movements).

5. Use a favorite pen or pencil and kind of paper.

6. Draft fast, if possible going from the beginning to the end of a segment without looking back (try to build momentum without worrying about grammar, punctuation, and spelling).

7. Do not write too long at one sitting lest the mind wander.

8. Put the draft away overnight, or longer if possible, to let it "cool."

9. Revise after the cooling-off period for content, checking with workpapers and outline; looking for mistakes in grammar, punctuation, and spelling; cutting; and reading aloud to test tone.

10. Ask a peer or co-worker who is unfamiliar with the specific subject but aware of the general framework to glance over the draft to detect loopholes or errors.

11. Proofread the typed copy.

These, among other steps, will systematize the task of writing and reduce the amount of revision by a supervisory colleague or professional editor. Systematization lessens the burden of writing, accelerating the issuance of a report and the sense of accomplishment which that entails. Without self-confidence, the inevitable difficulty of writing is magnified. With a systematic approach and with the techniques of style and organization available to all who have to write as part of their living will come the essential factor of self-confidence.

NOTES

[1] Ellsworth H. Morse, Jr., "Performance and Operational Auditing," *Journal of Accountancy*, vol. 131, no. 6, June 1971, p. 43.

[2] Albert Einstein and Leopold Infeld, *The Evolution of Physics*, Simon & Schuster, Inc., New York, 1967, p. xv.

[3] *Newsletter*, vol. 19, no. 10, Coopers & Lybrand, New York, October 1977, p. 3.

[4] Samuel I. Hayakawa, *Language in Thought and Action*, Harcourt Brace Jovanovich, Inc., New York, 1972, p. 156.

[5] American Institute of Certified Public Accountants, Management Advisory Services, *Guidelines for CPA Participation in Government Audit Engagements to Evaluate Economy, Efficiency and Program Results*, Guideline Series no. 6, New York, 1977, p. 50.

[6] Franklin N. McClelland, "Practitioners Forum," *Journal of Accountancy*, vol. 121, no. 4, April 1966, p. 71.

[7] James L. Ferguson, quoted in *The New York Times*, Dec. 10, 1976. © 1976 by The New York Times Company. Reprinted by permission.

[8] United States General Accounting Office, *Standards for Audit of Governmental Organizations, Programs, Activities, and Functions*, 1981 Revision, Government Printing Office, Washington, p. 17.

12 Reviewing drafts

A good audit report is usually the product of more than one hand. In any given assignment, a team of auditors may be involved. Special problems related to consistency then become apparent in the course of editing, revising, or rewriting. The purpose of dividing an audit assignment is to accelerate coverage and make the most productive use of varied expertise. Though the senior member of such a team bears the ultimate praise or blame, the drafter carries the initial responsibility. Many reviewers state that they lack self-confidence in critiquing a report. Yet they are charged with doing so, as in this statement from the Institute of Internal Auditors:

> Supervision includes: ... Making sure that audit reports are accurate, objective, clear, concise, constructive and timely.[1]

To be both efficient and productive, the members of an audit group should be clear as to their respective roles, responsibilities, and contributions. Accuracy of content is said by all involved to be their first concern, but the tone and style are inseparable from the content and may become issues between co-workers unless they are mutually resolved.

TEAM WRITING

What should be a valuable learning experience for the inexperienced members on a team may instead result in a sense of defeat. Drafters need to know the reason for changes. As one individual put it:

Three years ago, I liked to write. Now, after my style has been completely obliterated by my boss, it has become a drudge. I can no longer be objective about his comments.

As to reviewers, some feel that, as one expressed it:

Subordinates do not know how to write a report that is comprehensible by anyone else but themselves.

Drafters

A questionnaire given to drafters in large organizations contained this proposition: Do you like the writing you have to do? The majority of the responses was negative. Further comments indicated that the more extensive the review process, the greater the dislike for writing. Conversely, responses in smaller firms with little if any supervisory control over communications were preponderantly positive. In a situation where supervision does not extend to paperwork, the writer's attitude toward the task may be more favorable, but the quality of the finished product may suffer. One secretary said, with some misgivings, about the "boss": "He'll sign anything." An opportunity to learn is missed by the staff in such a case. In spite of all the complaints about revisions, almost every auditor answers "yes" to the question: Do you recall having been helped in your writing by a supervisor?

Reviewers, for their part, do not understand why obvious errors should abound in manuscripts submitted to them. In discussing qualifications, the Institute of Internal Auditors stipulates: "Internal auditors should be skilled in oral and written communications...."[2] One audit director said of the reviewing task:

It's the hardest part of the audit process.... Many times it is easier to start over than to make changes to the draft.

Another director commented:

To remake what one individual has started takes twice as long to correct as if I had done it in the first place.

When the drafters are not given the opportunity to be involved in making the changes, the same mistakes will be repeated. According to the General Accounting Office's *Standards* ..., the publication which is mandatory for federal auditors:

The most effective way to ensure the quality and expedite the progress of an assignment is by exercising proper supervision from the start of the planning to the completion of the report draft. Supervision adds seasoned judgment to the work done by less experienced staff and provides necessary training for them.[3]

Reviewers

Reviewers are themselves reviewed, all the way up the ladder, with the most biting comments coming from the top down. It has always been true that:

> Many executives have a strong tendency to become angry with clumsy wording, awkward phraseology, and confusing statements. Misspellings and grammar lapses drive them to apoplexy. Good writing requires more than fear to stimulate it, however.[4]

At its best, the relationship of the team members (including drafter, typist or word processing operator, and supervisory personnel at all levels) results in a clean, verified, acceptable, and convincing report. At its worst, the team relationship produces frustration.

The test is not the quantity of revisions but their quality, not how many changes can be made but how few will suffice. Frequently, there are too many levels of review. Time and team morale are at stake, and both are costly. In reality, the process extends all the way from basic editing to total rewriting. The most experienced staff members are the ones who demand the highest level of professionalism. Substantively speaking, they are the ones responsible for trends in the presentation of analytical and investigative reports. They are the ones most aware of the sensitivity of the situations undergoing examination. They are the ones who encourage or discourage their staffs when it comes to new approaches. Quality control, in other words, applies as much to a written product as to any other product.

Renewed emphasis upon fraud and abuse, as one illustration of a trend, involves high-level decisions about when and how initial information must be turned over to enforcement officials. In 1978, the Office of Inspector General, embracing the functions of audit, investigation, and analysis, was created in most federal departments.[5] This furthered the interaction of writers with varied specialties. When computer studies commenced, special reporting attention had to be exerted in data processing. Leadership in new directions starts at the top. To name another instance, when "auditing by objectives" was introduced by the head of a major agency, reviewers were then facilitated in checking the material submitted to them against the listed objectives.

Team authorship spanning both innovative and traditional approaches is more difficult than "sole source" authorship because preferences about writing are personal as well as professional. A long-time auditor expressed "uncertainty whether any correction I make is an improvement only in my own eyes." When reviewers talk to reviewees, these preferences can be explained. If there is no opportunity for discussion of changes in the wording of drafts, drafters fear the original meaning will be distorted. Such may be the case when a draft

is genuinely complex or ambiguous. Supervisory input entails adjustments ranging from word choice to the amount and arrangement of
factual support. As one reviewer commented:

> I am sometimes uncertain regarding the exact changes needed. It is easy to
> decide that I want a rewrite, but difficult to explain why or how.

For the writer who has labored over the draft and has conscientiously
exercised self-review, changes introduced without explanation often
appear to be mere prejudices. Revisions are interpreted, rightly or
wrongly, as impositions by someone higher on the organizational
chart and are perceived as the "prerogative of power."

Whatever the problems, a second look remains indispensable even
for accomplished writers. Good editing is not only accepted but
welcomed by published authors who are aware that their very
closeness to a subject may blind them to it. In the case of the careless
or hasty writer, supervisors are driven to wield that dangerous
weapon, the red pencil. One actual slip of the pen or mind (like the use
of "duplicity" when "duplication" was meant) can give the real
recipient an excuse to reject the surrounding content. Incorrect
arithmetic, outdated references, or sweeping assertions can be disastrous. Chaotic sequence, insufficient (or excessive) detail, unintended
innuendos, and antagonizing words will undermine credibility and
cooperation.

Though supervisors may receive drafts from persons who are highly
qualified as auditors, these persons may lack qualifications in the
discipline of the language. The supervisors themselves, no matter how
experienced in auditing, often feel equally lacking in the special
training necessary for good editing. One audit manager acknowledged: "I find I can see other people's mistakes better than my own."
Without a basis for mutual self-confidence in the team effort, interaction becomes difficult when attempted face-to-face.

Reviewers state that they read drafts first for accuracy of content,
then for objectivity of tone, and last (some say least) for style. That
order is sound if there are to be priorities in the process. The question
is whether content can be considered apart from the tone and the
style in which it is presented. In the final version, all three elements
become inseparable. When they mesh well, the writers, the reviewers,
and even the readers can take satisfaction in the end product.

VERIFIABILITY OF CONTENT

Reviewers of findings, intent upon testing for substance, look for
immediate disclosure of the problem, not only in the opening paragraph but in the first sentence of that crucial paragraph. The other
essential elements should then fall into place.

Essential elements

In the evaluation of a report, the five attributes of a "strong" (that is, a significant) finding are: condition, effect, cause, criteria, and recommendation. If the *condition* (the key point) is not self-evident, it will have to be ferreted out by digging through all the pages submitted for approval, sometimes through the workpapers themselves. Referencing drafts to workpapers is a basic step, the performance of which is usually taken for granted. But if the original writer has not probed in depth, the key point may not be there at all. Even if the analysis has been accomplished, the statement of the deficiency may not have taken shape on paper. Reviewers then have to prod their writers or put the point into words themselves. A basic decision may have to be made as to the significance of the facts. A drafted finding which does not identify the key point may be dropped entirely or incorporated with other items.

Discussion should take place before the changes become final, not only for verification but for purposes of teaching team members. It is natural for the writers to wonder what has happened to their efforts when they do not understand the reason for numerous emendations. They complain that their drafts are unrecognizable in the final product. At this point they may give up trying.

Second only to identification of the key point in the content as submitted is the reviewer's concern for a statement of *effect*. Questions that may need to be answered, especially in government audits, include these: Can a price tag be put on a particular discrepancy? Can inefficiency be calculated in terms of work hours or dollars to be saved or recouped? Is waste, extravagance, or actual fraud apparent? Has there been a failure to comply with regulations? Has a matter of opinion or inference been distinguished from a fact (that is, without a signal to the reader like "We believe. . . .")? Other safeguarding words like "not always" or "whenever feasible" are often the contribution of the more cautious supervisor who has learned to qualify sweeping assertions. ("All records were unavailable" becomes "Records were unavailable" or "Not all records were available.")

Investigators' reports undergo similar scrutiny but with another approach to content. Here, the obligation is to report facts more than to make judgments, so the drafters are generally precluded from inserting opinions unless the opinions are earmarked as such.

What any auditor-in-charge hopes to be able to identify in strong content, over and above condition and effect, is the *cause* of the problem. Until the reason for a deficiency can be pinpointed, the same situation may recur.

When noncompliance with *criteria* (regulations, precedents, policies, and procedures) exists, the problem is not hard to identify. Tangible standards of this kind are normally well presented by drafters, but reviewers must still determine how much of all such background is relevant. Drafters who have familiarized themselves with the entire situation incline to overwrite in this area. It is natural to cite applicable regulations at length. Cutting is then up to the reviewer, whereas careful paraphrasing in the first place might have produced the same result. Of course, it is easier for a reviewer to strike something out than to seek out and insert missing information.

Extremely important for supervisory checking are the *recommendations*. Proposed corrective actions must be matched against the deficiencies that have been disclosed. Weakly pointed, generalized statements deserve their label of "blue sky" recommendations. Reviewers also comment that weaknesses pointed out in an analysis are not always addressed completely in the recommendations that follow. It is equally possible that recommendations may address points that have not been established as needing correction. High among reviewers' complaints about content is lack of correlation between the action advised and preceding proof of need. The cost of implementing corrective steps also must be considered. Drafters are so close to their subject matter that loopholes in information or reasoning frequently become apparent only at the supervisory stage.

In any report, overall significance is the turning point. For that reason, minor problems are often consolidated into one basic problem. Such consolidation has to be based upon finding a single, underlying issue among different findings. The reviewer may be the one to discern what that unifying factor is. For the sake of substantiality rather than triviality, the report then presents various lesser issues as a single issue. Brevity as well as impact results from "single issue" reports.

One additional segment, the comments from the auditee (concurring or nonconcurring), is usually incorporated at the review stage. In cases of nonconcurrence, the auditor-in-charge prepares the response to the nonconcurrence for inclusion in the final report.

Factual support

The necessary level of factual support is another major review responsibility. Some auditors are instructed by supervisors: "Put everything in; I'll decide what's pertinent." The writer then misses the opportunity to exercise discretion or gain experience in selectivity. Field auditors who have been on the spot and have seen conditions firsthand may be inclined to put in every detail. Overkill results. The supervisors will see from their perspective that two examples instead of three, or one instead of two, will do. The opposite is needed when the drafter does not include adequate evidence, leaving gaps in the explanatory portion. If it comes to a choice, putting in too much is preferable to leaving out too much. Investigators particularly need help in setting forth all relevant facts (such as dates, places, and persons) instead of just those that point to the writers' own presumption of guilt or innocence.

Keeping in mind the frequency of loopholes in content, reviewers can be of special help. Have prior relevant audits been identified? Have the dates covered by the scope of the audit been specified? Are technical terms defined for the nontechnical reader? Does a statement regarding sampling reveal sample size and "universe," methodology of selection, and the confidence limits? Have potential monetary benefits been noted? Have projections of dollar amounts been labeled as such? The missing information usually exists in the mind of the initial presenter but may have to be dislodged and transferred to paper. Assumptions arising from familiarity are a natural hazard for those closest to the scene. All a supervisor has to do is to ask the right question, and the answer will be forthcoming. As one drafter suggested:

> Reviewers should make the writers use their own brains to clarify or reorganize by asking questions.

Incompleteness of content is one problem. Repetitiveness in content is another. Recipients of the final product, as well as supervisory readers, are critical on this score as well. To a certain extent, a prescribed format may induce restatement of the same point. The content of an opening summary is, for instance, redeveloped in the body of the document. The transmittal letter may itself summarize the summary. The table of contents consists of the headings that will reappear; these cannot be changed. Wording may be varied when standardized phraseology is not professionally prescribed. At each stage of a report's development, varied vocabulary instead of verbatim repetition can enhance the main points. Readers' comprehension and concurrence often necessitate reinforcement.

Professional approach

It is incumbent upon the reviewer to check for observance of all professional standards, including standardized wording when required, as enunciated by the American Institute for Certified Public Accountants (AICPA), the Institute of Internal Auditors (IIA), and the United States General Accounting Office (GAO). These standards, which are updated continually, require diligence on the part of every auditor but need reinforcement on the part of audit supervisors. To name one detail, the 1981 revision of the GAO *Standards*... reemphasized coverage of internal controls. Another update in the audit approach occurred when the United States Office of Management and

Budget in 1979 formulated for government activities the concept of the "single audit," which is still evolving.[6]

Once a draft has been checked for accuracy and adequacy of subject matter and fulfillment of current requirements, then comes consideration of the objectivity and fairness of the tone in which the content is represented.

ACCEPTABILITY OF TONE

Effective communication succeeds when the reader not only understands but is convinced by the points being made. Auditors, being by profession advisory in what they recommend, must depend upon persuasion. Flexibility is necessary. The tone of attack evokes defensiveness, which runs counter to the process of agreement.

One audit director expressed his responsibilities for "tonal quality" in these words:

> If the report does not motivate management in a positive manner to correct problems, we've failed! We've also failed when the problems are corrected in a negative atmosphere created by the report. For us (auditors) to be effective, we must work with and through management to achieve the stated objectives. The quality of the report plays a major role in creating the right working relationship with management.[7]

Balanced coverage

Field auditors who are closest to a situation focus necessarily on the facts as they see them and on their implications. They want to "tell it like it is." At times, such zeal may lead them to "overreach," or, as another experienced supervisor said, to "create findings." Unless the reporting of the facts and conclusions convinces an auditee as to their validity, communication has not taken place in the necessary sense of securing agreement. Auditors and investigators seldom are telling success stories. If problems exist, these evaluators report them. Gaining acceptance depends upon the way in which the problems are stated, especially when the problem amounts to criticism of the reader. Neither individuals nor organizations like to see their failures in print.

To make negative material more palatable, criticisms can, on occasion, be counterbalanced if writers give recognition to what has been done well. As a current trend affecting the tone of findings, the GAO *Standards . . .* now state that:

> The report shall: . . . Place primary emphasis on improvement rather than on criticism of the past; critical comments should be presented in a balanced perspective considering any unusual difficulties or circumstances faced by the operating officials concerned.[8]

Some auditors, trained to report by exception, are reluctant to include "significant management accomplishments." Yet the reporting requirements call for such information "to provide appropriate balance."[9] In rare instances, a whole finding or whole report may be positive; that is, it may reflect a situation where no deficiency was found.

Psychologically, the strategy of balancing the negative by the positive is conducive to securing agreement. A fair picture is a balanced picture, showing such strong points as are present together with the weak points. (In cases of fraud or abuse, the principle scarcely applies.) Being conservative by their professional nature, auditors are cautious about pointing to satisfactory or good performance lest another audit group should come upon an undetected weakness in the same activity. The advantages nevertheless outweigh the disadvantages in terms of demonstrating objectivity of tone that is conveyed by balancing the cons against the pros. As a statement by the Institute of Internal Auditors says:

> Auditee accomplishments, in terms of improvements since the last audit or in the establishment of a well-controlled operation, should be included in the audit report. This information is necessary to fairly represent the existing conditions and to provide a proper perspective and appropriate balance to the audit report.[10]

Criticism becomes more acceptable when accompanied by acknowledgment of "accomplishments" for others to see.

Subjectivity

Objective coverage requires objective wording. A good reviewer has to be on the alert for abrasiveness. Language that is inflammatory leads to resentment and resistance. When report-writers at any level allow their own sense of indignation to take over, however righteous that indignation may be, the wording becomes subjective:

> The obligation of [name of audited entity] to provide legally sound medical care is being seriously jeopardized when medications are dispensed.

Such wording, in the case cited, led to angry rebuttal and nonconcurrence at a headquarters level in hospital management, even though the facts were not disputed. The irate auditee declined to act on the report in a letter referring to "adversative proceedings." Subsequent review by the reporting staff led to the replacement of "legally" and "seriously jeopardized" with less threatening terminology. Concurrence was then forthcoming. Compromise in the mere wording did not necessitate compromise in the actual facts.

In another report, the reviewer found it easy to remove one word that might have precipitated an argument:

The number of qualified candidates from whom the official was selected was pitifully few.

"Pitifully" was deleted; the rest of the statement was accepted intact without further discussion.

The most glaring subjectivity, usually unconscious on the part of the firsthand writer but obvious to the more detached supervisor, is to be found in "repeat" audits. The drafter's wrath boils over when the recommendations agreed to a year or more ago remain unimplemented with no discernible change for the better. A candid restatement of the continuing condition, accompanied by reference to the earlier report and the updated observations, is needed in place of venting personal spleen. If such rewording still does not produce results, the reviewer may then invoke higher levels of management to seek compliance.

To be constructive does not mean to be bland. Watering down findings, which no ethical writer or reviewer wants, is different from toning them down. In removing the confrontational posture, the auditor's hope is for a winning strategy, not only for concurrence but for implementation. Acceptance is what leads to real rectification, not to the lip service of empty promises. Recommendations may have to be negotiated instead of imposed. After all, the auditor merely suggests. Management must direct, and the auditee must take the required steps. The wisdom of tact comes more naturally to writers who are reader-oriented, and many of those with the keenest reader-orientation are found among the team supervisors.

Reader orientation

Reviewers usually have the benefit of more professional experience than junior auditors. With experience comes greater awareness of the extended audience. Drafters are, understandably, content-oriented. When their content-orientation is matched by their reader-orientation, understanding by the intended recipient is more likely. "Getting newcomers to write in such a way as to convince the eventual recipient" was identified as the first task one auditor-in-charge faced.

Language itself should not be the source of argument (except for the calculated purpose of negotiation). If there is to be argument, it should center on the facts set forth in unemotional wording and on the logic of the conclusions drawn from the facts. A tone that is not combative is in line with the role of the report-writer who wishes to serve, not chastise. Style as a whole, going beyond mere word choice, is inextricably entwined with content as well as tone. In functional writing, style is the glove on the hand. The content then becomes actually the hand in the glove.

CORRECTNESS OF STYLE

If a report is to be taken as credible, the sentences, paragraphs, words, and punctuation marks must be correct; furthermore, they must readily communicate meaning. Style in literature may be important for its own sake; in analytical writing it is important for the sake of clarity. What the reviewer seeks is a style that is like a plate-glass window through which there is an unobstructed view of the content. As one reviewer expressed it:

> I try to respect the style of the writer and require changes where only the facts are compromised.

Editorial concerns

Carelessness in details of grammar obstructs the view and suggests to the reader carelessness in facts and reasoning. A reviewer cannot afford to let one misspelling slip by in a report. Editing for correctness, though no less essential in the review process than accuracy of content and objectivity of tone, calls for special skills. Those responsible for the quality of content and tone need a sharp eye when they receive drafts like these:

> Because of the attention that our disclosures recieved from the press and TV coverage; a copy of the report was officially released....

The semicolon (where there should have been a comma) broke the back of this sentence. The notorious misspelling of "received" betokens ignorance. Another internal audit report stated:

> Guidance for inflation of updated cost estimates for major systems was set-forth in a recent message. Instructions were to present all cost estimates in fiscial year 84 dollars (constant and escalated) with revised inflation indicies including the presidents salary. The cost estimate was not prepared using the perscribed indicies by january 1 84 for the next ficial year. The office which was responsible did not meet their obligations.

A reviewer's underlining in such a passage (as illustrated) should be enough to stimulate the faulty writer to consult a dictionary and rule book to make the corrections:

set-forth	= set forth
fiscial year 84	= fiscal year '84
constant and escalated	= possible jargon

presidents salary	= president's salary
perscribed	= prescribed
indicies	= indices (or indexes)
january 1 84	= January 1, 1984
ficial	= fiscal
their	= its (in reference to "office")

Word processing

Drafters and their seniors alike welcome all means of ensuring correctness, including the services of professional editors. Such special assistance is not widespread in audit teams. Occasionally, editorial skills have been provided by some well-trained secretaries, but such a resource is becoming less common. A new dimension of help in making revisions comes from word processing, that is, the use of technological equipment to speed up the process of writing. Reviewers' changes can now be made much more quickly. Developments in automating the writing process are proceeding so rapidly that the real writers, at all levels, have to think and move fast to keep abreast. In the face of the electronic devices, some may feel like giving up, signing off, dropping out, or even retiring. Yet writers having important things to say will seize all opportunities to help themselves.

Word processing is a computerized method for preparing dictated or handwritten communications for issuance in completed form. By means of a typewriterlike, electronic keyboard and a built-in display screen, either the operator (often the secretary) or the originator transfers material to the screen (soft copy, and easy to change). The screen has been likened to "reusable" paper. On the screen itself, the revisions may be typed in by striking coded keys or by striking over the letters to make corrections. The revisions are much more easily inserted or substituted than on traditional typewriters. Deletions are equally easy to make. Whole paragraphs or sentences ("blocks") may be manipulated or a mere typographical error may be corrected.

Facilitating revisions has so far proved to be word processing's chief asset in the preparation of functional communications. Once the finished draft appears on the screen (sometimes a television screen serves the purpose), that version may be fed automatically into a printer, which instantly turns out the final copy or copies. The messages are put onto small, circular, magnetic-coded records ('floppy disks") for storage.

In this ongoing automation of certain aspects of writing, the advantages have already been recognized and welcomed. Standardized formats (that is, patterns) can supply uniformity in many respects including margins, indentions, forms for figures (as in dates or dollars), use of capital letters, and typography in general. There are some cautions as well:

1. Writers must learn the mechanics of word processing; they must not be intimidated by the keyboard, screen, printer, internal processing unit, or disk, or by the jargon itself; and they must work with the operating staff to keep up with the mechanized resources. The word processing vocabulary is the initial hurdle because it consists of new words (like "cursor"), new uses of old words (like "daisy wheel" or "columnar wrap"), or new acronyms (like "ROM" for "Read only Memory"). To minimize the jargon, "user-friendly" language that can be generally understood is being developed for high-level, nearly conversational programming.

2. Writers who do become familiar with the process must anticipate delays in output until sufficient, synchronized equipment becomes available in the office for word processing to live up to its reputation for speed. The printer may, for instance, become overloaded with "print" requests, thereby causing the very kind of delays it was designed to prevent. A mix of word processing systems within a given organization may complicate matters.

3. Hopeful writers must not expect any equipment, no matter how sophisticated, to do the thinking and the drafting. That process (the mental burden) remains the function of the human mind. The writer will remain the originator and the reviser will remain responsible for whatever emerges from the computerized system. Many promotional statements need to be taken with a grain of salt. One news release stated:

> If a wordy writer types "at this point in time," a computer program will suggest a substitute: "now." It also will detect split infinitives and sexist phrases, tally the number of sentences written in the passive voice and, if need be, flash a warning on a screen that "passive sentences are harder to understand than active sentences."[11]

There is no magic, but there is help. Word processing can, it is true, open whole new worlds when keyed to such data bank sources as color graphics, stored formats, electronic mail, foreign language translations, and even voice messages. Those who have already adopted this equipment as part of their office life say that the system gives back just what it takes in. The process, like any data processing device, does not think or exercise discretion. When it comes to the rudiments of spelling and punctuation, "packages" of limited adaptability can be purchased, but unanticipated questions or exceptions to the rule will not be caught. Proofreading is no less necessary than before, perhaps more so.

There is, in other words, no total mechanized solution for the human process of communicating convincingly. From the rigors of thinking and transferring thought to paper, there is no escape. Word processing will assist writers but will not fill the need for better style and organization. If properly incorporated into the day's routine, the system will, however, facilitate the performance of the human task.

The human eye will still see farther than any automated adjunct. The capacity to err in communicating is not completely foreseeable, as this example showed:

Changes in the coming year's methods of distributing copies are eminent.

When spelling goes by ear ("eminent" for "imminent"), correction by the editor is imperative, whether the material is handwritten or dictated. A dictated statement concerning "heirs at law" came back from the word processor as "errors in law." Handwriting itself may require human deciphering, and handwriting is the first form of transmission for many who have to work "on location," away from their own offices.

Traditional grammar

Traditional grammar is the preference of experienced reviewers who want observance of the "rules of the road." Clarity and acceptability alike suffer from too much experimentation, from what some describe as "picturesque" style. Complete sentences (not telegraphic) with identifiable pronouns, agreement between singulars and plurals, properly placed modifiers, parallelism, and accurate tense sequence are the means to clarity. Experimental usages deserving close editorial scrutiny include the pyramiding of nouns (to serve as adjectives) on top of nouns and other freewheeling changes of words that once were nouns to verbs ("to format," "to impact," "to dimensionalize") or vice versa ("an update"). Airline agents on occasion agree to "overnight" their passengers. But language goes by precedent as well as innovation, and the reviewer is, by experience, more attuned to readers' resistance to change in the matter of language as well as in substantive matters.

Even when correctness has been ensured, original drafts have to be made easy to read. Simple, not simplistic, communication is the goal. A sentence may be correct yet require rereading. The reviewer can then attempt to improve the style.

Cutting superfluous words (particularly modifiers like "very," "quite," "various," and "somewhat") is usually possible. Reducing sentence length by decoupling (replacement of "and" by a period) is frequently an easement. Dividing long paragraphs or inserting subparagraphs is another boon for the intended recipient. When such measures do not begin with the original drafter, the auditor-in-charge must undertake the task, and so on up the ladder until clarity and flow are achieved. The major problem one middle-level auditor acknowledged was "wondering if my revised versions will make it through the next level."

ROLES OF WRITERS AND REVIEWERS

Auditors whose overall job performance is routinely evaluated now find their writing receiving conspicuous attention. Some audit directors use actual score sheets and grade the quality of the reports submitted to them. The ability to communicate well has become a highly visible asset in both industry and government. Often included on appraisal forms is a section in which the supervisor is required to comment on communication skills. Because written communications are tangible evidence pro or con, writing is frequently singled out for comment.

Self-review

Strict self-review is the first step to take. A drafter needs to let material "cool" overnight. If the drafts are read aloud, problems will be heard by the ear (like sentence length) that are not caught by the eye. Informal peer-group review is also an advantage, freeing the participants from the inherent fear of supervisory disapproval. Not only peer review is useful, but also review by subordinates. There are supervisors who request comments or criticisms from their juniors.

Drafters, at whatever level, are many times dissatisfied with the way their thoughts look when transferred to typescript. As an indispensable step, either before or after typing, self-review is worth the time it takes. The need for corrections is easier to see in a typed copy. Self-reviewers can be the best reviewers. They know exactly what they want to say. If a total rewrite seems indicated, they can go back to the drawing board. If substantial emendation seems called for, they should be the first to fill the need. In completing a self-review before submitting the draft, proofreading is an absolute obligation of the author in order to correct even minute imperfections that would otherwise catch the eye of the auditor-in-charge.

Assumptions in team writing

Once rigorous self-review has been finished, team play takes over. First, what are the difficulties in this system of team writing for the original writers? Many do not foresee that:

- Changes may be made, often without discussion, by a succession of reviewers.
- Numerous levels of review may be built into the system.
- Different supervisors may inject their own preferences, differing from the preferences of other supervisors.
- Tone may be altered either up or down the scale of severity.

- Content may be rearranged when the whole report is "packaged," with major deletions, additions, or substitutions.
- Format may look different.
- Original meaning may undergo distortion.
- Findings may be combined or eliminated.

These are problems that can at least be anticipated and, if so, alleviated.

What are the difficulties in team writing for the reviewers? Many of them do not foresee that:

- The necessity for teamwork may not be the automatic expectation of the drafter.
- Drafts may be submitted with glaring errors in grammar, spelling, and punctuation.
- Self-review may not be carried out by the author.
- Frustration may result from unexplained revisions (sometimes to the extent of undermining general cooperation).
- Demoralization may be a side effect.
- Discussion may be needed before the correct sense emerges in cases of ambiguity.
- The attitude and tone conveyed to the intended recipient may undergo unintentional softening or hardening.
- Delays in issuance may be prolonged beyond deadlines by the extent of review.

Constructive initiatives

In bringing the roles of writer and reviewer into alignment, some teams of report writers have already demonstrated initiatives. The planners' steps include these:

- Hold initial discussions of the coverage of a given report, including all to be involved and directing attention to any survey or audit guide. Outline possible findings in advance, assigning sections to team members.
- Explain the functions of reviewers all along the line, including the eventual "packaging" of the whole document in accordance with the prescribed format.
- Check the progress of individual drafters at intervals to prevent overwriting (or underwriting); to point out any emerging inconsistencies in format, tone, or style among different team members; and to lend encouragement.
- Look for a statement of the condition (the key point as analyzed) and for cause, effect, criteria, and potential recommendations.

- Compile a "point sheet" listing these attributes where warranted.
- Spot-check workpapers in relation to drafted paragraphs.
- Adapt the tone to fit the situation being disclosed.
- Incorporate balancing factors in accordance with GAO *Standards*....
- Edit for details of grammar.
- Indicate where and why revisions are needed, leaving the actual revision up to the originator.
- Reinforce drafters' self-confidence by pointing out strong points, not only the weak ones.
- Make the actual corrections only when the originator is unable to do so, giving reasons in terms of common sense. (If the grammatical rules cannot be explained, as may be the case, the reviewer should either say so frankly or let well enough alone.)
- Curtail changes attributable to personal preference but acknowledge those that are so attributable for what they are. (Everyone has individual tastes.)
- Reduce the number of review stages, shortening the process and avoiding revision of revisions.
- Submit a reviewed draft to the auditee, when tactically desirable, as an "exposure draft" for preliminary reaction.

Idealistic as such practices seem to hard-pressed evaluators working against the clock, lack of time should not be an excuse for unacceptable reports. Timeliness itself will suffer from uneconomical review practices that are unnecessarily extensive or intensive. Only if the roles of writers and reviewers alike are reassessed can the self-confidence of the drafters be raised and the burden upon the reviewers be reduced.[12]

The requirements of team writing may cast a shadow over an individual's chance to write as an individual. Herein lies the frustration for the individualist who becomes part of a group whenever a personally prepared draft is rewritten, sometimes minimally, sometimes beyond recognition. The supervisor may change a mere word, but it is a knife to the heart. This sensitivity to personal preferences regarding vocabulary runs high. The writer may look upon unexplained word changing by a senior as the imposition of prejudice, the altering of sentences as nit-picking, and the revising of content as distortion of facts. The writer has struggled to turn out a good draft; it has not been easy. Good writing seldom is. Changes hurt.

One trainee in a public accounting firm was asked how a supervisor could be most helpful about report preparation. The trainee replied:

> By creating an atmosphere that does not threaten the author's intelligence, capability, or competence.

The most experienced reviewer, on the other hand, finds it necessary to make the report "fail-safe" and to anticipate the objections and misgivings of the ultimate recipients. A state audit director explained his technique this way:

> I normally require the draft to sit on the shelf for at least a day before releasing the exposure draft to management prior to an exit conference. Just prior to releasing the report to management, my last review becomes a role-playing exercise. I attempt to play the role of management in order to determine how I would react if I were receiving the report.[13]

If the tone is accusatory, it can be translated into one of objectivity. If organizational sensitivities are exposed to inflammatory imputations, detachment can be supplied. Indignation need not show through the writing. Another undeniable value lies in the clarification which may be achieved by mere correctness of the language. If a draft is overloaded (or underloaded) with detail, there is even greater need for help.

Usually, more than one reviewer is involved before a report reaches the issuance phase. There are times when the personnel originally assigned to do the reviewing may change (transfer or resign, perhaps). Revisions may be made at each rung of the organizational ladder. Then, only the "view from the top" will bring the picture into focus. Different findings are often drafted by different individuals, making scissors and paste or the "cursor" as useful to the reviewer as a pencil. Consistency has to be provided from the supervisory level if the authorship is multiple. In the final document, unity is expected by the reader, especially at the start and at the close. In the words of one who knew, a barbershop quartet is different from solo singing.

In the course of this often painful process of team writing, pride of authorship dwindles. Yet without room left for self-gratification, the effort of drafting will itself slacken. The solution lies in accepting the concept of collective authorship, in the course of which writers and reviewers aim to remain in continuous touch. The best of such relationships becomes a self-learning, confidence-building experience. Career incentives to write well are strong. In the conjoint approach to report-writing, the development of communication skills becomes part of the entire process of developing rather than inhibiting professional talent.

NOTES

[1] Institute of Internal Auditors, Inc., *Standards for the Professional Practice of Internal Auditing*, Altamonte Springs, Fla., Third Printing, 1979, pp. 200–201.

[2] Ibid, pp. 200–202.

[3] United States General Accounting Office, *Standards for Audit of Governmental Organizations, Programs, Activities, and Functions,* Government Printing Office, 1981 Revision, Washington, p. 36.

[4] Frederick C. Dyer, "Managing Other People's Writing," *Management Review,* vol. 51, no. 2, February 1962, p. 45.

[5] *Inspector General Act of 1978,* Pub. L. 95–452, 92 Stat. 1101 (1978), codified and amended, 5 U.S. Code Annotated, App. I, West Publishing Company, St. Paul, Minn.

[6] U.S. Office of Management and Budget, *Attachment P,* Audit Requirements to OMB Circular A-102, "Uniform Administrative Requirements for Grants-in-Aid to State and Local Governments," Washington, 1980, pp. 2101–2138. Also contained in *Federal Register,* Oct. 22, 1979, vol. 44, no. 205, pp. 60958–60960; proposed revision in *Federal Register,* Aug. 8, 1983, vol. 48, no. 153, pp. 36030–36032. See also: H. J. Steinberg, J. R. Miller, and T. E. Menzel, "The Single Audit in Government," *Journal of Accountancy,* vol. 151, no. 6, June 1981, pp. 56–66. See further: Arthur Andersen & Co., *Auditing of Grants, The "Single Audit Concept,"* Chicago, April 1982. (Pamphlet.)

[7] Letter to author, 1983.

[8] GAO, *Standards . . . ,* pp. 6–11.

[9] Ibid, p. 53.

[10] Institute of Internal Auditors, Inc., Professional Standards and Responsibilities Committee: *Statement on Internal Auditing Standards, No. 1* from *Exposure Draft, Communicating Results.* (Passage approved.) Altamonte Springs, Fla., 1983, p. 9.

[11] *The Wall Street Journal,* Nov. 8, 1982, p. 31.

[12] See "Checklist for Reviewing Report Drafts," Appendix, pp. 199–200.

[13] Letter to author, 1983.

Appendix

CHECKLIST FOR REVIEWING REPORT DRAFTS

If both self-reviewers and supervisory reviewers follow a step-by-step procedure for reviewing drafts, they will have an insurance policy for the improved quality of their reports:

1. Is the drafting proceeding on schedule (that is, in accordance with a timetable if one has been set)?

2. Have the audit organization's own guidelines (including matters of format like title page, table of contents, transmittal, executive digest, and the introductory components of purpose, scope, and background) been followed?

3. Has the draft been read from beginning to end without pencil in hand for overall substance and then reread with pencil in hand (not a red one) for editorial corrections and other types of improvements needed?

4. Have acronyms been held to a minimum and spelled out initially?

5. Have numbers been treated consistently (that is, in accordance with a policy related to the use of words or digits)?

6. Has jargon (special or technical terms) been avoided or defined as necessary?

7. Have graphics (like tables, charts, diagrams, and photographs) been used if suitable?

8. Has each attachment (appended item) been labeled and referred to in the body of the report?

9. Has the distribution been clearly marked as restricted or otherwise?

10. Has the use of statistical sampling been explained (as, for instance, sample and population size, method of selection, and confidence level)?

11. Have dates been given for the period which the audit covered and the period when audit work was performed?

12. Have monetary factors (benefits or excesses) been considered for dollar impact?

13. Has material indicating possible fraud been turned over to investigative or legal authorities?

14. Have either the American Institute of Certified Public Accountants or General Accounting Office standards been observed in the case of public accounting firms or governmental agencies, respectively?

15. Have all the stated objectives of a given audit been addressed?

16. Do the findings generally include "condition," "cause," "effect," "criteria," and "recommendations"?

17. Do the recommendations correlate with the deficiencies?

18. Have any "noteworthy accomplishments" of the audited entity been mentioned as desired?

19. Have corrective actions (or the lack thereof) mentioned in a prior audit been indicated?

20. Have the auditee's own comments been requested and received before issuance? If adverse, have comments been responded to by the auditor?

21. Is the copy free of errors in grammar, spelling, and punctuation?

22. Finally, has the reviewer's annotated copy of the draft been discussed with the writer so that the writer has been given the chance to make or verify the necessary changes?

Selected reading references

American Institute of Certified Public Accountants: *Codification of Statement on Auditing Standards*, no. 1-44, New York, 1983.

———: *Suggested Guidelines for the Structure and Content of Audit Guides Prepared by Federal Agencies for Use by CPAs*, New York, 1972.

———, Committee on Governmental Accounting and Auditing: *Industry Audit Guide—Audits of State and Local Governmental Units*, New York, 1981.

———, Management Advisory Services: *Guidelines for CPA Participation in Government Audit Engagements to Evaluate Economy, Efficiency and Program Results*, Guideline Series no. 6, New York, 1977. (Note the bibliography therein.)

Arthur Andersen & Co.: *Auditing of Grants, The "Single Audit Concept,"* Chicago, April 1982. (Pamphlet.)

Brink, Victor Z., and Herbert Witt: *Modern Internal Auditing: Appraising Operation and Control*, 4th ed., John Wiley & Sons, New York, 1982.

Broadus, W. A., Jr., and J. G. Moraglio: "Governmental Audit Standards: A New Perspective," *Journal of Accountancy*, vol. 153, no. 5, May 1982, pp. 80–86.

Bromage, Mary C.: "Accountants and the Written Word," *Singapore Accountant*, vol. 5, Singapore, 1970, pp. 9–13.

———: "Auditors' Jargon," *Internal Auditor*, vol. 27, no. 6, November-December 1970, pp. 63–67.

———: "Reporting of Management Audits," *Federal Accountant*, vol. 20, no. 4, December 1971, pp. 72–82.

———: "Reports Are More than Words," *U.S. Army Audit Agency Bulletin*, vol. 465-24, Spring 1968, pp. 34–40.

———: "The Wording of Audit Reports," *Internal Auditor*, vol. 40, no. 1, February 1983, pp. 36–38.

————: "Wording the Management Audit Report," *Journal of Accountancy*, vol. 133, no. 2, February 1972, pp. 50–57.

Burton, John C.: "Management Auditing," *Journal of Accountancy*, vol. 125, no. 5, May 1968, pp. 41–46.

Cancellieri, Alfred, and Darryl Enstrom: *The Expanded Scope of Government Auditing*, Coopers & Lybrand, New York, 1976.

Carmichael, D. R.: "Some Hard Questions on Management Audits," *Journal of Accountancy*, vol. 129, no. 2, February 1970, pp. 72–74.

Cashin, James A., ed.: *Handbook for Auditors*, McGraw-Hill Book Company, New York, 1971.

Davis, Keith: *What You Should Know about Administrative Communication*, Indiana University, Bureau of Business Research, Bloomington, March 1954. (Pamphlet.)

Defliese, Philip L., Kenneth P. Johnson, and Roderick K. MacLeod: *Montgomery's Auditing*, 9th ed., The Ronald Press Company, New York, 1975.

Dittenhofer, Mortimer A.: *Concepts of Governmental Auditing*, Institute of Internal Auditors, Inc., Altamonte Springs, Fla., 1978.

Eifler, Thomas A.: *Performing the Operations Audit*, American Management Association Extension Institute, 1974.

Fowler, Henry W.: *A Dictionary of Modern English Usage*, 2d ed., Ernest Gowers (ed.), Oxford University Press, New York, 1965.

General Accounting Office: See entries under United States General Accounting Office.

Gowers, Ernest: *The Complete Plain Words*, Her Majesty's Stationery Office, London, 1973.

Granof, Michael H.: "Operational Auditing Standards for Audits of Government Services," *CPA Journal*, vol. 43, no. 12, December 1973, pp. 1079–1088.

Graves, Robert, and Alan Hodge: *The Reader over Your Shoulder*, The Macmillan Company, New York, 1961.

Guttman, Daniel: *The Shadow Government*, Random House, Inc., New York, 1976.

Hall, Edward T.: *The Silent Language*, Doubleday & Company, Inc., Garden City, N.Y., 1973.

Hayakawa, Samuel I.: *Language in Thought and Action*, Harcourt Brace Jovanovich, Inc., New York, 1978.

Hunter, Laura Grace: *The Language of Audit Reports*, Government Printing Office, Washington, 1957.

Institute of Internal Auditors, Inc.: *Standards for the Professional Practice of Internal Auditing*, Altamonte Springs, Fla., 1978.

————, Professional Standards and Responsibilities Committee: *Statement on Internal Auditing Standard No. 1, Communicating Results*, Altamonte Springs, Fla., 1983.

Kierzek, J. M., and Walker Gibson: *Handbook of Writing and Revision*, The Macmillan Company, New York, 1967.

Kropatkin, Philip: "How to Write an Audit Finding," *Footnote*, The Department of Health, Education, and Welfare Audit Agency, Atlanta, August 1980, pp. 19–23.

Lindberg, Roy A., and Theodore Cohn: *Operations Auditing*, American Management Association, New York, 1972.

Lowe, James: *9,000 Words: A Supplement to Webster's Third New International Dictionary*, Merriam-Webster Inc., Springfield, Mass., 1983.

McLuhan, Marshall: *Understanding Media*, McGraw-Hill Book Company, New York, 1973.

Mair, William C., Donald R. Wood, and Keagle W. Davis, partners, Touche Ross & Co.: *Computer Control & Audit*, Institute of Internal Auditors, Inc., Altamonte Springs, Fla., 1978.

Mautz, Robert K., Alan G. Merten, and Dennis G. Severance: *Senior Management Control of Computer-Based Information Systems*, Financial Executives Research Foundation, Morristown, N.J., 1983.

Mints, Frederic E.: *Behavioral Patterns in Internal Audit Relationships*, Institute of Internal Auditors, Inc., Altamonte Springs, Fla., 1972.

Morse, Ellsworth H., Jr.: "The Expanding Role of the Auditor in Government Operations," speech, Oregon, 1971. (Mimeographed.)

————: "Performance and Operational Auditing," *Journal of Accountancy*, vol. 131, no. 6, June 1971, pp. 41–54.

Newman, Edwin: *Strictly Speaking* and *A Civil Tongue*, Warner Books, Inc., New York, 1980.

Norbeck, Edward F.: *Operational Auditing for Management Control*, American Management Association, New York, 1969.

Norgaard, Corine T.: "The Professional Accountant's View of Operational Auditing," *Journal of Accountancy*, vol. 128, no. 6, December 1969, pp. 45–48.

Northrup, C. S. (ed.): *Essays of Francis Bacon*, Houghton Mifflin Company, Boston, 1908.

Pierpont, Wilbur K.: "Program Review and Evaluation in the Business and Financial Area," *Studies in Management*, vol. 3, no. 1, National Association of College and University Business Offices, Washington, July 1973.

Robertson, Jack C.: *Auditing*, Business Publications, Inc., Dallas, 1976.

Roget's *University Thesaurus in Dictionary Form*, Berkley Publishing Corp., New York, 1978.

Secoy, Thomas G.: "A CPA's Opinion on Management Performance," *Journal of Accountancy*, vol. 132, no. 1, July 1971, pp. 53–59.

Simonetti, Gilbert, Jr.: "Auditing Standards Established by the GAO," in "Washington Report," *Journal of Accountancy*, vol. 137, no. 1, January 1974, pp. 33–39.

Staats, Elmer B.: "GAO Auditing in the Seventies," *GAO Review*, Spring 1972, pp. 1–10.

————: "Governmental Auditing in a Period of Rising Social Concerns," address, Nassau, 1972. (Pamphlet.)

————: "How Can We Increase Confidence in the Management of Federal Programs?" Economic Club of Detroit, Mich., Nov. 26, 1973. (Pamphlet.)

————: "Management of Operational Auditing," *GAO Review*, Winter 1972, pp. 25–35.

Steinberg, H. J., J. R. Miller, and T. E. Menzel: "The Single Audit in Government," *Journal of Accountancy*, vol. 151, no. 6, June 1981, pp. 56–66.

Stepnick, Edward W.: "Audit Findings—Their Nature and Development," *Footnote*, Department of Health, Education, and Welfare Audit Agency, Atlanta, August 1980, pp. 15–18.

Strunk, William, Jr., and E. B. White: *The Elements of Style*, 3d ed., The Macmillan Company, New York, 1978.

United States General Accounting Office: *Additional GAO Audit Standards—Auditing Computer-Based Systems*, Government Printing Office, Washington, 1979.

————: *Auditing Efficiency, Economy and Effectiveness in Government*, Government Printing Office, Washington, June 1974.

————: *Auditors: Agents for Good Government*, Government Printing Office, Washington, 1973. (Pamphlet.)

————: *Examples of Findings from Governmental Audits*, Government Printing Office, Washington, 1973. (Pamphlet.)

————: *from auditing to editing*, Government Printing Office, Washington, 1974.

————: *Internal Auditing in Federal Agencies*, Government Printing Office, Washington, 1974.

————: *Monthly List of General Accounting Office Reports*, GAO, Washington. (Issued monthly.)

————: *Questions and Answers on the Standards for Audit of Governmental Organizations, Programs, Activities & Functions*, Government Printing Office, Washington, 1974.

————: *Standards for Audit of Governmental Organizations, Programs, Activities and Functions*, Government Printing Office, 1981 Revision, Washington.

United States Government Printing Office: *Style Manual*, Government Printing Office, Washington, 1972 (reprinted in 1979).

United States Office of Management and Budget: *Attachment P to OMB Circular A-102*, "Uniform Administrative Requirements for Grants-in-Aid to State and Local Governments," Washington, 1980.

————. *Audit of Federal Operations and Programs; Revision, Circular No. 17–73*, Washington, 1978.

United States Senate, Subcommittee on Reports, Accounting and Management of the Committee on Government Operations: *The Accounting Establishment*, Government Printing Office, Washington, 1976.

————, Subcommittee on Reports, Accounting and Management of the Committee on Governmental Affairs, *Improving the Accountability of Publicly Owned Corporations and Their Auditors*, Government Printing Office, Washington, 1977.

Watson, A. J.: "Do Financial Statements Communicate?" *The Accountant's Magazine*, vol. 72, Edinburgh, May 1968, p. 236.

Webster's Third New International Dictionary, Unabridged, 3d ed., Merriam-Webster Inc., Springfield, Mass., 1981.

Witte, Arthur E.: "Management Auditing: The Present State of the Art," *Journal of Accountancy*, vol. 124, no. 2, August 1967, pp. 54–58.

Yeager, L. C. J., and Gordon Ford: *History of the Professional Practice of Accounting in Kentucky*, Courier-Journal Lithographing Company, Louisville, Ky., 1968.

Index

About the Author

Mary C. Bromage is professor emerita of written communication, Graduate School of Business Administration, The University of Michigan. She is a frequent lecturer and consultant on written communication for national business firms and federal agencies, and she has conducted workshops throughout the United States, Canada, and Europe, as well as the Far East, the Middle East, Latin America, and Africa.

The Department of Commerce Interagency Auditor Training Center recently chose her for its annual award of merit as "the most outstanding instructor at the Center" and elected her to its Hall of Fame. Professor Bromage is the author of *Cases in Written Communications, Writing for Business, Churchill and Ireland,* and *DeValera and the March of a Nation,* as well as scores of articles in professional and academic journals.